A Divided People

CONTRIBUTIONS IN AMERICAN STUDIES

Series Editor   Robert H. Walker

Art and Politics: Cartoonists of the *Masses* and *Liberator*
Richard Fitzgerald

Progress and Pragmatism: James, Dewey, Beard, and the American Idea of Progress
David W. Marcell

The Muse and the Librarian
Roy P. Basler

Henry B. Fuller of Chicago: The Ordeal of a Genteel Realist in Ungenteel America
Bernard R. Bowron, Jr.

Mother Was a Lady: Self and Society in Selected American Children's Periodicals,
1865-1890
R. Gordon Kelly

The *Eagle* and Brooklyn: A Community Newspaper, 1841-1955
Raymond A. Schroth, S.J.

Black Protest: Issues and Tactics
Robert C. Dick

American Values: Continuity and Change
Ralph H. Gabriel

Where I'm Bound: Patterns of Slavery and Freedom in Black American Autobiography
Sidonie Smith

William Allen White: Maverick on Main Street
John D. McKee

American Studies Abroad
Robert H. Walker, Editor

American Studies: Topics and Sources
Robert H. Walker, Editor

In the Driver's Seat: The Automobile in American Literature and Popular Culture
Cynthia Golomb Dettelbach

The United States in Norwegian History
Sigmund Skard

Milestones in American Literary History
Robert E. Spiller

KENNETH S. LYNN

A Divided People

Contributions in American Studies, Number 30

GP GREENWOOD PRESS
WESTPORT, CONNECTICUT • LONDON, ENGLAND

Library of Congress Cataloging in Publication Data

Lynn, Kenneth Schuyler.
  A divided people.

  (Contributions in American studies ; no. 30)
  Includes bibliographical references and index.
    1. American loyalitsts—Biography. 2. United States—History—Revolution,
1775-1783—Biography. 3. United States—History—Revolution, 1775-1783—
Causes. I. Title.
E277.L96   973.3'092'2 [B]   76-25779
  ISBN 0-8371-9271-4

Library of Congress Catalog Card Number: 76-25779
ISBN: 0-8371-9271-4

First published in 1977

Greenwood Press, Inc.
51 Riverside Avenue, Westport, Connecticut 06880

Printed in the United States of America

For my instigators
A. S. L.
E. L.
S. L.

A man's relation, for instance, to his father . . . may de-termine the pattern of his later political conduct or of his intellectual preoccupations without his being in the least conscious of the connection. . .

—SIR LEWIS NAMIER, **Personalities and Powers** (1955)

Contents

Acknowledgments

I am very grateful to Oscar Handlin and to Robert H. Walker for their careful readings of my manuscript, and for their imaginative suggestions as to how I could improve it. I also wish to thank Jack P. Greene for many instructive conversations about colonial American history. Finally, I wish to pay tribute to a brilliant essay by Edwin G. Burrows and Michael Wallace, "The American Revolution: The Ideology and Psychology of National Liberation" (*Perspectives in American History*, 1972), which gave me the confidence to pursue the study of individual human lives that I have attempted here.

A Divided People

Loyalist Backgrounds

In the Declaration of Independence, Thomas Jefferson spoke of "one people," but his brave words concealed a very different reality. Perhaps as many as 20 percent of the 2.1 million white people living in the colonies on the eve of the war opposed independence and favored reconciliation with Great Britain. In the words of a contemporary observer, "Nabour was against Nabour."[1]

Why did the colonists respond in such dramatically different ways to the efforts of the British to reform the management of their empire? What were the underlying dissimilarities between apparently like-minded neighbors that led to the transformation of some of them into political revolutionaries and of others into fifth-column agents of the Crown? I recently went through the literature of Revolutionary biography with these puzzling questions in mind, but failed to find completely convincing answers, even though most of the books I was reading contained enlightening descriptions of the social, political, and economic pressures to which their heroes had been subject. Clearly, something was missing.

It was not difficult to figure out, once I thought about it, that what these books suffered from was a lack of curiosity about the childhoods of the men they were purporting to explain. About external influences on adult behavior I had been told a great deal; about the psychological formation of adult personality I had been told strikingly little. Had the future patriot and loyalist leaders been close to their parents in their formative years, or alienated from them? When tension had flared between the generations, how had it been resolved? Had the fathers been strong or weak role models for their sons? At what age had the sons left home, and how had their parents felt about their departure? It was remarkable how uninterested most biographers were in exploring such vitally important issues. Psychologically speaking, the average Revolutionary biography was about as deep as a children's comic book.

Yet the psychological shallowness of the average biography made those studies which had shown at least some awareness of the importance of childhood stand out in my mind, and caused me to realize that they composed contrasting patterns: the patriots and the loyalists who were the central figures in these books had undergone rather different sorts of experience in their early years, especially in relation to their fathers.

I am aware that the crossroads at which psychology and politics meet is, to paraphrase a famous sentence of Lionel Trilling's, a dark and bloody place that is constantly being raked by critical fire from all sides. To venture out there is regarded by a good many people as a foolhardy act under any conditions. To venture out there with a new theory about that most cherished of all American events, our national origin, may very well be interpreted, even by some of my friends, as a sign that poor Lynn has gone crazy. Sane men, after all, do not ask for trouble. Nevertheless, I have written this book, because I could not stop thinking about the implications of my evidence.

In this chapter and the one that follows, I propose to illustrate by means of capsule biographies the differences I have observed between the patriots and the loyalists, and to formulate the questions those differences raise. Then in the third chapter I hope to persuade my readers that, unlike some psy-cho-historians of justly ill repute, it is not my purpose to strip history of its complexity, but simply to demonstrate that we need to add another pattern to that beautifully rich mosaic which is the story of the American Revolution.

A final warning. The following biographies are not balanced accounts, in the manner of the entries in the *Dictionary of American Biography*. They are weighted so as to serve my special purposes.

BENEDICT ARNOLD took an awful chance when he went back on the oath of American allegiance he had pledged at Valley Forge. Yet as his biographer, Willard M. Wallace, points out, there were complicated emotions at work in Arnold that finally overrode his reasons for keeping the Revolutionary faith. Like the Reverend Jacob Duché and a number of other colonists, Benedict Arnold recanted his initial decision to break with Britain in defiance of prudential considerations. The feelings that drove him to do so are traceable to his childhood.

An earlier Benedict Arnold had been a wealthy man and the governor of Rhode Island. Unfortunately, his son, also named Benedict, suffered such grave financial losses that he was compelled to apprentice his own son and namesake to a barrel maker. Eventually Benedict III left Rhode Island for Norwich, Connecticut, where he not only prospered as a cooper but did well in investments in coastal and West Indian shipping. His marriage to Hannah King, the widow of a well-to-do merchant, enabled him to put barrel making behind him and become a sea captain and importer. Captain Arnold's ships brought molasses, sugar, and rum to New England, and handsome profits to the ex-cooper. With his earnings Arnold purchased a splendid house, in which he entertained the local gentry. He won a number of political offices. Dreaming dynastic dreams, he also sired six children, only to have four of them die. His namesake son, however, turned out to be a superbly healthy child.

In the late 1740s business fell off disastrously. Benedict III sought comfort in the rum he was importing but not selling. Soon he found himself in the grip of a habit he could not shake. Although he would outlive his wife, he was a drunkard for the remainder of his days.

The sudden deterioration of his father turned young Benedict into an alarmingly disobedient child, and the more that Captain Arnold withdrew from the life of the family into an alcoholic haze, the wilder the boy became. As Willard M. Wallace observes, "If he had had a father capable of guiding him, one whom he could have admired and emulated, he might have learned restraint. Unfortunately, there was little to admire or copy in his father during the very years when Arnold needed a firm hand." His mother was increasingly apprehensive about her son's behavior, but was unable to control it by herself. Finally she sent him away to school in Canterbury, Connecticut, when he was eleven. It was her hope, she told the Reverend Dr. James Cogswell, the headmaster of the school, that he would not spare the rod and spoil the child. Three years later, Benedict was abruptly removed from the school. His father's condition had grown appallingly worse, and the family's financial resources were nearing exhaustion.

Freed from Cogswell's punitive rule and contemptuous of his mother's admonitions to behave himself, Benedict joined forces with other juveniles who enjoyed making life miserable for the neighbors. Inasmuch as he was stronger than the other boys, a faster runner, and a far more daring prankster, Benedict easily became their leader, but ultimately his audacity led him into the arms of the town constable. His worried mother now decided that the discipline of an apprenticeship was the only thing that could save him. Accordingly, she dispatched him to an apothecary shop run by her cousins.

At seventeen the youth ran away and joined the militia in New York. When his mother appealed to the authorities, he was sent home. A year later, however, he reenlisted. Within two months his regimental commander listed him as a deserter. That same year, 1759, his mother died. Arnold responded to the event with a series of incoherent gestures. He rejoined the army, but only briefly. Taking to the sea, he wandered the Atlantic world from England to the West Indies. His life utterly lacked direction, and the death of his father in 1761 left him feeling more rootless than ever. Yet his father's passing also filled him with a sense of relief. For the senior Arnold's public drunkenness had never ceased to be a source of anguish to his son. Not surprisingly, young Benedict was already noted for his moderate drinking habits, as well as for his invariably angry reaction to the drunkenness of others. In many other respects, though, he was a most immoderate young man, and the death of his father did nothing to calm him down.

The outbreak of fighting in 1775 thus represented a great opportunity for Arnold, in that it furnished him with a socially respectable outlet for his wildness and violence. With Ethan Allen he captured Fort Ticonderoga. He stopped the British thrust from Canada down Lake Champlain. He helped to compel Burgoyne's surrender. By 1778 he was a major general in command of forces at Philadelphia. He at last had recouped the traditional high standing of the Arnolds.

When, however, he was threatened with a court-martial for various irregularities, he could not stand the prospect of public humiliation. Moreover, he was convinced—not without reason—that the military establishment was treating him with gross injustice and disrespect. He therefore entered into secret correspondence with the British. Another consideration that may have influenced this fateful act was his inordinate appetite for money, of which he never had enough. It is also quite possible that his wife, a well-born Philadelphian with a host of prominent loyalist friends, spurred him on with caustic comments about the social inferiority of the officers who were sitting in judgment upon him. But behind all of the circumstances that goaded him toward the betrayal at West Point, there lurked the sorry history of his upbringing. In the summary judgment of Willard M. Wallace, Benedict Arnold constituted

> a pathetic case of insecurity. He had to be first in all things, and in nothing could he be wrong. In the terrible pride of the general was the pride of the boy who had been the daredevil among his friends, the strongest of arm and fleetest of foot. In the officer who sought respectability in wealth and in marriage into one of the first families of Philadelphia was also the high-strung lad who had chafed under the humiliation of a drunken father. All his life he pursued respectability and acceptance by "first families" as a social equal. Unfortunately one of his obsessions was that riches ensured respectability and that the means by which those riches were gained was immaterial. The result was that to obtain respectability as he conceived of it, he constantly resorted to devices that jeopardized his objective and made his honor as a "gentleman" a mockery. . . . Needing money sorely in the spring of 1779, and confronted with public disgrace as a consequence of the . . . impending court martial, he looked for reassurance. Where else could it more surely be found than among the British, who would welcome his assistance and pay handsomely for it?[2]

JONATHAN BOUCHER came from a family which, like Benedict Arnold's, had been eminent in an earlier generation, but had subsequently suffered a loss of status. Again like Arnold, Boucher grew up in the knowledge that his father was a drunkard. Family pride and family shame mingled in young Jonathan's soul, and emerged as a desperately insecure snobbery. All his life he would revere wealth and power, even though that reverence would cost him everything he owned in the mid-1770s and send him destitute into exile.

The Bouchers had once owned large properties in the county of Cumberland in the north of England, but in the course of the seventeenth-century wars had lost them all. Thereafter the family never rose above the yeoman class. Indeed, the death of Boucher's paternal grandfather at the age of twenty-four plunged his widow and three growing children into poverty. When a cabinetmaker from Dublin asked her to marry him, the young widow had little choice but to consent. The marriage, Jonathan Boucher remarked many years later in his amazingly frank *Reminiscences of an American Loyalist,* was "not a happy match." The cabinetmaker's inability to earn a decent wage magnified the unhappiness of Boucher's grandmother, as did the strangeness to her of life in Ireland. In her self-pity, she regarded the children of her first marriage as "eyesores," and quickly apprenticed James, the eldest, to a shoemaker.

James Boucher made a seemingly advantageous marriage at a young age. His bride was a widow named Walker from Kilkenny, with good connections and a tidy inheritance. Backed by his wife's money, James became a tradesman, with thirty employees. But he was not successful. "A lively facetious man," he sang a good song, loved company, and was always in company. In the end he paid his creditors twenty shillings on the pound and took his wife across the Irish Sea to the Bouchers' bleak point of origin in the town of Blencogo in Cumberland County. The lady from Kilkenny hated the remote and backward place even more than James did, and she soon grew "fretful and quarrelsome." To get away from her shrewishness, James began to "live almost constantly in ale-houses." His financial reserves, such as they were, dwindled every time he raised a mug. The fatal illness of his wife finally solved the problem of the Bouchers' unhappiness. On her deathbed she is reputed to have acknowledged that she had taken pleasure in James's difficulties, and had, in fact, "by plan and on purpose, endeavoured to accelerate his approaching ruin." If he had spent his last penny, he might have taken her back to Ireland.

Two daughters were born of James's first marriage, both of whom he sent off to live with relatives after his wife's death. With the coast clear, he then married Anne Barnes, the daughter of a widowed housekeeper. According to their son's *Reminiscences*, "This was not an equal and therefore not a very happy match." Anne Boucher was a good woman, her son condescendingly admitted, but inasmuch as her origins were lowly, she had, "as was natural, low notions, which my father, naturally warm and high-minded, . . . [but] now soured by his undone circumstances, too often thought lower than they really were." "He should have recollected," Boucher bitterly added, "that they never could be too low for the situation to which through his misconduct he was now reduced." Warming to the task of excoriating James's irresponsibility, the author of the *Reminiscences* then asked why a man of his father's great capacity and abilities ever tried to retrieve his fortune in so wretched a place as Blencogo. To which question the author replied that "It must have been owing to his having by this time contracted low habits of thinking along with the low and vulgar habit of tippling and drunkenness." His mother, Boucher implacably continued, "had but one object in view, and one plan of attaining it. She was anxious to reclaim her husband, and to be able to maintain their rising family; and she hoped to effect this by unwearied industry and the most rigid frugality." But no amount of dedication on Anne Boucher's part could pull her husband out of the swamp of his ruined life.

Part of the problem was that James and Anne set up an alehouse, which put James directly in the path of temptation. When he was not drinking up his profits, he taught school and farmed a parcel of land that the family still owned, but his labors had indifferent results. All in all, his son estimated, James earned no more than fifteen pounds a year, on which he had to raise four children. "We lived in such a state of penury and hardship," Boucher recalled, "as I have never since seen equalled, no, not even in parish almshouses." Despite their poverty, his parents managed for a time to send Jonathan to a third-rate school. Although the masters were obviously incompetent, the boy was eager to learn what he could from them. But in the end this episode merely left him with something else to complain about. "As though it had not been enough to place me under bad masters, . . . I was not even permitted to attend them with constancy." Heedless of his protests, his parents compelled him to leave school and go to work. He carted coals, turf, and peat, drove a plow, cut hay, and harvested grain. For years, he "worked as hard as any man in England and, I may add, fared as hard."

In the aggrieved tone that dominates Boucher's narrative of his early life speaks the voice of a boy who did not like anything about his situation, and who very much wanted to become someone else. His first chance to escape into a new identity was offered to him by a gentlewoman named Thomlinson, who lived in a large house called The Hall at the other end of Blencogo. This high-minded, domineering woman fascinated the unhappy boy. She had no children of her own, and seemed, moreover, to be "unsuitably married." He reveled in the attention she lavished upon him. When he was about eight years old, however, his fantasy of becoming Mrs. Thomlinson's heir was rudely shattered by the announcement that she was expecting a baby. In time, she gave birth to two sons. Although she still continued to invite Jonathan to the house and to give him presents of money and clothes, going to see her was never again as exciting as it once had been. Even so, he remained enduringly grateful to her for exposing him to a better life. "Before I was twelve years old," he says in his *Reminiscences,* "I had resolved I would not pass through life like the boors around me." In Mrs. Thomlinson's house, the young Boucher saw "a little something that looked like genteel life, and which, while it inspired me with some taste and longing for it, rendered me not quite so awkward and uncouth as I must needs have been without it."

Shortly before he realized that his benefactress intended to betray him by having children of her own, the boy experienced another revelation that was equally shattering. The news of Mrs. Thomlinson's pregnancy left him feeling more lonely than ever; the sight of the decapitated bodies filled him with fear. When Jonathan was seven years old, the invading Highland armies of the young Pretender passed within a few miles of Blencogo. The next year, the impressionable boy was taken—probably by his father—to witness the execution of the leading Jacobite rebels, whose skulls for many years afterward adorned the walls of Carlisle. Certainly there were many other factors in Jonathan Boucher's early life that conspired to make him respectful of regal authority figures. But perhaps the traumatic spectacle of what could happen to men who dared to rebel against a king was sufficient in itself to freeze his loyalty.

Jonathan's second chance to acquire a new identity occurred in 1755, when he was eighteen. Despite the inadequacy of his education, he was obviously bright, and in an interview for a position as a tutor and minor functionary at a school in St. Bees, he talked the headmaster, the Reverend John James, into hiring him. At twenty-six, John James was still a young man, and his wife, Ann, was only twenty-three. But in spite of their youth, Jonathan instantly looked upon them as the parents he had been searching for. Even their names were uncannily right for the surrogate roles he wished them to play, for the headmaster's surname was the same as his real father's Christian name, while the Christian names of Ann James and Anne Boucher differed only in spelling. So starved was he for all the cultural amenities that the Jameses took for granted in their daily life that he accepted everything they told him. Indeed, his surrender to them was so total that they may very well have been uneasy about it. Yet there is no doubt that they returned his affection in ample measure. Under John James's direction, he filled in some of the gaping holes in his education, and Ann James sympathized with his seemingly manic-depressive cycles of enthusiasm and discouragement. If he had come to them earlier in his adolescence, he might eventually have worked through his dependency on them. Instead, the Jameses simply taught him how wonderful it was to be supported by external authority.

In 1758, his surrogate parents encouraged him to accept a position as a private tutor in Virginia, and he agreed to do so, despite his extreme reluctance to leave them. His letters to John James from the New World reveal a continuing dependency, as well as a terrible sense of dislocation. Send letters by every ship, he implored the headmaster, for "I know how little I am able to bear interruptions [in my correspondence]." "Drop all reserve," he pleaded. "I have often found you too gentle in rebuke. Be so much my friend as to be in appearance my enemy: trust me, I'll look upon it as the greatest instance of your regard for me." The weather in Virginia appalled him, and so did the people. He was "stunned and stupefied" by the coarseness of American manners, as well as by the bawdiness of masculine conversation. "Libertinism," he announced disgustedly, "is the reigning topic." Americans thought of him as "splenetic and grave," and that was how he felt. Nothing went right in this accursed land. Shortly after taking a promising job as a clerk, his employer, a certain Captain Dixon, asked his help in arranging his marriage to a wealthy widow. For a fee, Dixon wanted Boucher to swear that he was the father of one of the captain's illegitimate children. When Boucher indignantly refused, he lost his position. With his funds running low, he borrowed money from John James, thus increasing his sense of inadequacy.

He finally adjusted to the New World by imitating John James's career. Although he had never been notably devout, he took Anglican orders, accepted the call to a church, and started a school. Most of his pupils were "the sons of persons of the first condition in the colony," he proudly noted. "Jacky" Custis, for example, was the son of Mrs. Martha Washington and the stepson of George. Boucher worked hard at the social connections that his tutoring opened to him, and eventually they paid off. In 1770, his influential friends helped him to become the rector of St. Anne's in Annapolis, an appointment which he had been angling for for several years.

Boucher's opinion of Annapolis was that it was the "genteelest town in America." With an eagerness born of his ineradicable feelings of deprivation, he plunged into its social life, campaigned successfully for the presidency of its leading literary club, and cultivated an intimacy with Governor Eden. Here was another sun to bask in. Soon Boucher was using his position as chaplain of the lower house of the Assembly to make himself politically useful to Eden. He drew up speeches and messages for the governor, as well as some of the Council's important papers, while on the floor of the House he became the unofficial manager of legislation. "Hardly a Bill was brought in," he later boasted, "which I did not either draw or at least revise." At the time of the Stamp Act he had denounced British policy in a letter to John James as "in every Sense, oppressive, impolitic & illegal," but the idea of rebelling against imperial power was so unthinkable to him that it never once crossed his mind. In his Annapolis years he composed polemics attacking the Whig radicals who were harrassing Governor Eden, his fatherly protector.

In gratitude, Eden bestowed on him the highly desirable rectory of Queen Anne's Parish in Prince George's County. Shortly after receiving this plum, Boucher married Eleanor Addison, who brought him a sizable dowry and a new father figure to look up to. The sense of well-being that Boucher felt in the presence of his wealthy father-in-law revealed his continuing needs. "Mr. Addison . . . is my James in America," he exultantly wrote to John James.

Some months after the wedding, the clergyman installed his bride in a plantation house with a fine spread of property overlooking the Potomac. Counting five or six white servants, there were almost seventy people on the place. But Boucher was to enjoy his new position as a landed gentleman for less than three years. As the political crisis intensified, he kept loaded pistols handy in the pulpit while preaching his pro-British sermons, until the pressure on him became intolerable. Abandoning everything, he returned to England in 1775, where he eked out a living for almost two decades as vicar of Epsom.

Shortly before he died, he wrote a book on the *Causes and Consequences of the American Revolution*, in which he made it clear that he had always thought of loyalty to one's king as a form of father worship. "The leading idea, or principle, of Sir Robert Filmer's Patriarcha is, that government is not of human, but divine origin; and that the government of a family is the basis, or pattern, of all other government. And this principle, notwithstanding Mr. Locke's answer, is still . . . unrefuted, and still true." Where America had gone wrong was in forgetting that "Kingdoms and empires are but so many larger families." Even now, Boucher concluded, "I cannot dissociate the idea of a perfect sameness of interest between the two countries, as much as between a parent and a child."[3]

MATHER BYLES was born in Boston, the son of Josias Byles, a man he never knew. By his first marriage, Josias had eight children, whom he was hard put to raise on his earnings as a saddle maker. In 1704, following his wife's death, he married for a second time. He was forty-seven and his new wife, Elizabeth, was thirty-seven or thirty-eight. Elizabeth gave birth to a son in 1707, but her marital happiness was short-lived; within a year her husband was dead. There being not much money in the estate, she was forced to turn to her father and brother for assistance—which they were in a position to provide, because her father was Increase Mather and her brother the redoubtable Cotton. In marrying Elizabeth, Josias had established a connection considerably above his own station in life. The infant Mather Byles represented a union of two different levels of Boston life.

Grandfather Increase died when Mather Byles was seventeen. The old Puritan willed a fair-sized sum of money to his daughter Elizabeth, with the explicit hope that she would use it to further the education of her intellectually promising son. In addition, he left the youth his wearing apparel and one fourth of the books in his library. Increase also called on his son Cotton to be "a father to a fatherless child," and to "take care of ye education of ye child as of his owne." In the final clause of his will dealing with his grandson, Increase said that he fervently desired and prayed that the young man would enter the ministry.

Increase's admonition to his son to act in loco parentis to Byles was totally unnecessary, for Cotton Mather had long since been conscious of the role he had to play in his nephew's life. On April 15, 1711, not long after the boy's fourth birthday, Cotton had noted in his diary, "I must be much of Father to the fatherless child of my Sister Biles. One thing I particularly now propose; that I will give him the little Book of 'Good Lessons for Children,' and give him a Piece of Money for every one of the lessons that he learns without a Book." Cotton was also concerned that the boy might die of consumption, and he constantly cautioned him to take care of his health.

But even if the boy had been the picture of health, Cotton still would have hovered over him, intervening in every aspect of his activity and counseling him at every turn in his development, for that was Cotton's compulsive way with children. In *Bonifacius. An Essay Upon the Good*, Cotton informed the parents of the English-speaking world that unless they were in "a continual agony" to do for their children "all the *good* that ever you can," then they were "without *bowels*." He thereupon set forth a twenty-point list of parental resolutions which reveals a good deal about the sort of father he himself was. On the one hand, he tried very hard to avoid "that harsh, fierce, crabbed usage of the children, that would make them tremble, and abhor to come into my presence."

On the other hand, he was so fearfully anxious for the young to lead Christian lives that he could not bring himself to let them alone so that they could learn by trial and error. "I would be solicitous," runs a typical resolution,

> to have my *children* expert, not only at *reading* handsomely, but also at *writing* a fair hand. I will then assign them such *books* to *read*, as I may judge most agreeable and profitable; obliging them to give me some account of what they *read*; but keep a strict eye upon them, that they don't stumble on *the Devil's library*, and poison themselves with foolish *romances*, or *novels*, or *plays*, or *songs*, or *jests that are not convenient*. I will set them also, to *write* out such things, as may be of the greatest benefit unto them; and they shall have their blank books, neatly kept on purpose, to enter such passages as I advise them to. I will particularly require them now and then, to *write* a *prayer* of their own composing, and bring it unto me; that so I may discern, what sense they have of their own everlasting interests.

There is no evidence that Mather Byles ever objected to this sort of control. Throughout his youth he seems to have been completely in awe of his uncle, and humbly eager to please him, as if by doing so he might become, like his cousin Sam, the real son of Cotton Mather, During his undergraduate years at Harvard, Byles's behavior continued to be flawless. Judge Sewall's report on the student body in 1723, which asserted that many undergraduates stole, lied, swore, picked locks, drank, and were idle, did not reflect on "virtuous and studious" Mather Byles. Upon graduation, Byles was one of only two members of the class of 1725 who went on to the ministry. In a period of religious declension, the youth dutifully took up the calling that his grandfather Increase had wanted him to.

Although Byles "shared unmistakably," in his biographer's words, "in the peculiar mental temperament of his uncle," he was intellectually more royalist than the king. Where the brilliant Cotton restlessly pursued learning in a hundred different directions, Byles was content with a narrowly traditional erudition. As for his sermons, they were emphatically Old Calvinist, never betraying the least hint of Hopkinsianism, the slightest tendency toward Unitarianism, or any other taint of innovation.

Inevitably he made advantageous marriages, for he did not allow himself to be interested in eligible women who did not have prominent fathers. His first wife was the daughter of a wealthy physician and a niece of Governor Belcher, with whom Byles cultivated a close friendship. His second wife was as well connected as her predecessor. Not only was her father twice Lieutenant Governor of Massachusetts, but she was related to a number of the most aristocratic families in Boston. Through his cousin Sam, who married a sister of Thomas Hutchinson, the socially indefatigable clergyman widened his circle of influential acquaintances still further.

It has been asserted that Byles's marital and social connections were responsible for his Toryism. While the assertion is undoubtedly true, there is a deeper truth about Byles, which is that the origins of his loyalism were located in a personality which forever required the approval of authority figures on the highest level of Massachusetts society. There were many Bostonians who did not care for Mather Byles, because of his air of superiority. Beneath the clergyman's hauteur, however, lay nervousness and immaturity. At Byles's trial in 1777 for disloyalty to the state, young John Eliot irritatedly observed that the old man was "a silly, impertinent, childish *person*." What prompted Eliot's remark was Byles's incorrigible habit of punning, even when he was giving sworn answers to grave charges. His reflexive habit of finding everything amusing was, like his superior airs, a defense mechanism, which he had been employing all his life. Perhaps it was their consciousness that Byles was not only old but pathetic which at the last moment prompted Revolutionary officials to commute his sentence of exile to England or the West Indies. He spent his remaining days confined to his house.[4]

DANIEL DULANY was heartily despised by many of his fellow Marylanders. Not only did they disapprove of his scurrilously ad hominem attacks on his political opponents, but they were put off by his vain and haughty personality. Yet as Robert McCluer Calhoon has observed, Dulany's haughtiness was the outward manifestation of an exhausting inner struggle to apply himself to the stewardship of the exalted place in Maryland society and politics that his father had prepared for him. Daniel Dulany, Jr., lived a life that had been programmed by Daniel Dulany, Sr., and the program was not easy.

The elder Dulany was born in Ireland, in 1685. Although his father, Thomas Dulany, had very little money, he wanted his son to become an educated gentleman. Accordingly, he sent Daniel to the University of Dublin. But unlike the other students, Daniel was forever running short of cash. When the situation finally became "uneasy to him," he dropped out of the university and emigrated to Maryland.

It took the penniless Irish redemptioner only nine years to become a wealthy Charles County lawyer and the husband of an heiress whose dowry included vast estates. Life was sweet, but after a cruelly short twelve months, it turned sour. Squire Dulany's wife died, and her plantations reverted to the estate of her late father. The disconsolate Irishman decided to leave Charles County and start life anew in Prince George's County.

Once again he got ahead. Once again he married well. Soon he was a familiar figure in the society of the county's ruling families. Yet he had a feeling of uncertainty about his new eminence. When short tobacco crops brought financial difficulty to Maryland planters in the 1720s, Dulany's law practice dropped off badly. Having suffered a hard fall from a great height once before, he did not need this reminder that disaster could strike again at any time.

Dulany's sense of the precariousness of life made him an extraordinarily cautious politician. When he finally fulfilled his ambition to become attorney general of Maryland, he did not use his position to stir up the passions of the electorate or to organize demonstrations in favor of great causes. Aubrey C. Land points out in *The Dulanys of Maryland* that Daniel Dulany, Sr., avoided any sort of involvement in the tobacco-cutting riots and other "dangerous noveltys" which in his view threatened peace and stable government in Maryland. Although he was in a position to do so, he never called into question the proprietary rights of Lord Baltimore.

A stubbornly persevering man, the elder Dulany was determined that his son and namesake would follow in his footsteps and solidify his gains. He had Daniel, Jr.'s whole career mapped out in his mind. He would go to Eton. After Eton he would go to Cambridge. After Cambridge he would enter the Middle Temple. After the Middle Temple, he would come back to Maryland, hang out his shingle, enter politics, and become rich and powerful. A letter from the senior Dulany to the Reverend Peter Godard, his son's tutor at Cambridge, indicates who was calling the signals in Daniel, Jr.'s life: "As I design him for the law, I am very glad to hear that he attends your lectures diligently. . . ."

The younger Dulany entered Eton at thirteen and returned to America at twenty-five, after completing his studies at the Middle Temple. In many respects, his career habits closely resembled his father's. If the older Dulany doggedly kept moving toward his goals, so did the younger. Yet where the father was cautious, the son was rigid and tense. His sense of strain became even more pronounced after his father died. Having always been dutiful, he apparently missed being commanded. Thus in the spring of 1757, four years after his father's death, he suffered the first of two mental breakdowns which caused his family to fear for his life.

In his writings in the 1760s, Dulany opposed the Stamp Act. But unlike the firebrands who talked of open defiance and organized resistance, Dulany called for discreet protest and submission. Those in authority, after all, had to be obeyed.[5]

WILLIAM FRANKLIN had everything to gain, from a materialistic point of view, by following his father into the Revolutionary camp, and everything to lose by remaining loyal to a British ministry that obviously had no further use for him. The calculations, however, of the illegitimate and marginally talented son of a world-renowned genius were not governed by a cool assessment of where his advantage lay, but by an irrational yearning.

He was born in 1730. His mother in all likelihood was not Deborah Read, but whether or not they were blood relations, she was not fond of him. Benjamin Franklin's clerk, Daniel Fisher, was staggered by the foul invective employed by Deborah when she spoke of William. Fisher's theory was that she was jealous of him, because her husband preferred his son's company to hers. Certainly Benjamin Franklin treated William with more consideration than Deborah did. He recognized the boy as his son, took him into his household, and raised him to be a gentleman. If the elder Franklin was far too busy with his multiple enterprises to be an attentive parent, he displayed an indulgent affection for the boy whenever they were together. Yet the very amicability of the father increased the agony of the son. There was a terrible frustration in William Franklin that circumstances did not permit him to express.

Thanks to his father's influence, William was appointed in his young manhood to several minor posts in the Pennsylvania government. Later he accompanied the elder Franklin to England, where he studied law at the Middle Temple. In 1762, William was awarded an honorary M.A. by Oxford on the occasion when his father received an honorary doctorate of civil laws. Through the intervention of Lord Bute, William also was commissioned governor of New Jersey in 1762, but once again the honor came to him because of his father. By naming William to an important post, Bute hoped to persuade the elder Franklin to look favorably on his ministry. William never achieved anything on his own, and William knew it. No matter where he turned, he stood in the shadow of the colossal reputation of Benjamin Franklin.

As governor, then, William was very anxious to establish a separate identity of his own. Unfortunately, he possessed neither a brilliant mind nor a commanding physical presence nor a charming personality, and his administration was utterly undistinguished. While granting that the American colonies had real grievances, he refused to recognize that they had any right to plead their case outside regular imperial channels. In his illegitimacy, Governor Franklin was a stickler for legitimate procedures. Even the little band of lawyers, merchants, and office holders who made up the governing elite of New Jersey seem to have found him stuffy.

In 1776 he chose to remain loyal to the Crown, despite the scorn of his father, who disgustedly characterized William as "a thorough courtier." The decision should not surprise us. For if William Franklin had joined his father in crossing to the Revolutionary side, he once again would have become lost in shadow. His choice of loyalism was the desperate effort of a middle-aged man to declare his personal independence.[6]

THOMAS HUTCHINSON, the last civilian royal governor of Massachusetts, was born in Boston in 1711. The fourth of twelve children, he was brought up in a household that was family oriented to an extraordinary degree. His father, Colonel Thomas Hutchinson, was a prosperous merchant and ship-owner who loved nothing better than to spend his money improving the splendid town house which was the Hutchinsons' home. Colonel Hutchinson had inherited the dwelling from his widowed Aunt Abigail, and it was typical of the family's intricate genealogy that Aunt Abigail's third husband, John Foster, who had built the house, was also the father by a previous marriage of Sarah Foster, who became Colonel Hutchinson's wife. A further entanglement between the Fosters and the Hutchinsons resulted when Colonel Hutchinson's half-brother Edward married another of John Foster's daughters.

Sarah Hutchinson was ten years older than her husband, which raises the question of whether Colonel Hutchinson had been looking for the security of a mother when he took a wife, for his own mother had died within a year of his birth. Whatever his matrimonial motive, Hutchinson was an intensely domestic husband. When his wife began having children the year after they were married, he played his paternal role with the utmost seriousness. Thus the colonel read the Scriptures to his assembled offspring every morning and every evening, seven days a week. The number of outsiders whom he permitted to penetrate the family circle was very small. On Saturdays, the colonel regularly invited four close friends, two of whom were relatives, all of whom were merchants like himself, to dinner. Occasionally a clergyman was also invited, but no other additions to the guest list were ever made. In the Hutchinson mansion, life unfolded in fixed and orderly routines, which no stranger was allowed to disrupt.

The personal tragedies that struck the family only caused the survivors to draw more closely together, as did the financial losses that significantly reduced the Hutchinsons' wealth. Foster, the eldest of the children, *"a most lovely son,"* died in 1721 at the age of seventeen; his death, his younger brother Thomas remembered, was a particularly "heavy stroke" to their father. Four other children died in infancy. Then in 1739, Elisha, the third oldest son, succumbed to a fever, aged twenty-three. The loss broke the colonel's spirit, and he fell into what his son Thomas described as "a languishing illness." Within a year he was dead of a "hectic fever."

As the younger Thomas Hutchinson did not fail to note, his father's fatal fever was only the concluding episode in a long history of illness. All his life the colonel suffered from "indigestion and flatulencies at his stomach," which may have been the symptoms of a psychological illness. For in later years the colonel experienced "two or three turns . . . of nervous disorders, which confined him several weeks at a time and deprived him of his sleep." If Colonel Hutchinson did not invite Boston society into his house, it was not simply because he was a devoted husband and father who preferred to be alone with his family. It was also because his nervous temperament required a tranquil setting and familiar faces.

"Caution, control, and prudence," says Bernard Bailyn, were the "guiding principles" of Governor Thomas Hutchinson's life. Governor Hutchinson himself admitted with a wry candor that "my temper does not incline to enthusiasm." If he had a passion, it was for the traditions of bygone years. He loved history, especially the history of Massachusetts, and most especially the history of his own family. All the time he was an undergraduate at Harvard, so he said about himself half a century later, he "kept a little paper journal and ledger, and entered into it every dinner, supper, breakfast, and every article of expense, even of a shilling, which practice soon became pleasant, and he found it of great use all his life. . . ." In Benjamin Franklin's case, this kind of attention to his own activities was a form of boasting, but in Hutchinson's case it was primarily a means of imposing an order upon experience. By focusing attention on the most minute details of his own behavior, he was able to blot out the strange and possibly upsetting behavior of others. Hutchinson also had a political habit of appointing relatives to important offices, which was taken by his enemies as proof of what a Machiavellian schemer he was. But the governor spun his webs for psychological as well as political purposes. His nepotism, like his narcissistic diary entries, enabled him to stamp his own image on an alarmingly alien world.

Hutchinson's neurotically rigid upbringing, which was the source of his social nervousness, also turned him into a worrier about his physical health. In 1762, he began to follow a program of careful eating, regular exercise, and restricted work hours. Nevertheless he suffered a nervous breakdown in the spring of 1767, from which he recovered only gradually. In the words of Bernard Bailyn, "he was never thereafter free of worry about himself as well as about the world."

His refuge, like his father's before him, was his family. Hutchinson's marriage to Margaret Sanford in 1734 flowered into a partnership of remarkable closeness. He also found a sense of security and well-being in fatherhood. (He sired twelve children, the same number that Colonel Hutchinson had.) Whenever he came home, he was happy. Margaret's death in childbirth in 1754 was therefore a shattering blow; it cost him, he cried, more than half his soul. For years thereafter he shunned all social activity, using his children as a protective shield to keep well-wishers at bay. Of the five children who survived infancy, he was closest to the youngest, whose birth had led to his wife's death. He named her Margaret, after her mother, and called her Peggy, as he had his wife. Peggy lived with her father as companion and secretary until she died at the age of twenty-three. She apparently never thought of marriage, even as he had no desire to take a second wife.

The three Hutchinson children who married were scarcely more independent-minded than their sister. In a remarkable display of Hutchinsonian solidarity, they all married in the early 1770s into the Oliver family. This multiple alliance between two of the most prominent Tory families in Boston had important consequences in the emerging revolutionary struggle. But the chief significance of these marriages lay in what they revealed about the collective psychology of the Hutchinsons. For two generations, the family had shown a marked tendency to withdraw into itself. That tendency had now become pathological. Perhaps the turning point in the Hutchinsons' fear of the outside world had come in 1765, when a Boston mob sent them fleeing from the supper table, and then wrecked the lovely mansion that had been their sanctum for half a century. Thereafter the Hutchinsons seemed deeply frightened by anything strange, to the point where the children could marry only Olivers, if they married at all.

As for Governor Hutchinson and the American Revolution, the thought of political independence terrified him, for it too represented novelty. In his alarmist frame of mind, he was sure that America could not possibly survive in a world of warring nation-states. A man who cherished the familiar as much as he did was clearly not made for exile, yet exile became his fate. In England he predictably failed to adjust to new conditions, and died yearning for the land of his birth.[7]

WILLIAM SAMUEL JOHNSON was one of the makers of the Constitution of the United States, although he had firmly opposed the Declaration of Independence.

According to his biographer, George C. Groce, Jr., the most important factor in forming Johnson's character was his father, the Reverend Samuel Johnson, rector of the Anglican church in Stratford, Connecticut. A descendant of Congregational ministers, Samuel Johnson had converted to Anglicanism as a result of falling passionately in love with all things English. He had visited England in 1722 and was enthralled by its ancient civilization. Thereafter he looked upon the land of his birth with disdain. Its people were uncouth, its institutions immature, its culture virtually nonexistent. America was merely a child; England was a parent.

Following his return to Connecticut, Johnson married a widow with two sons. In 1727, William Samuel was born. His father at once dedicated the boy to the service of the Lord.

This dedication not only propelled William Samuel into a program of religious training, but into the literary and legal study of his English heritage. As his son's principal teacher, the Reverend Mr. Johnson firmly believed in the adage, "Train up the child in the way he should go, and when he is old he will not depart from it." At age four, the boy received regular assignments in a primer. By the time he was eight, he had read the catechism of the Church of England more times than he could remember, was familiar with Aesop and Virgil in translation, and had commenced the study of Latin. At ten, he was well on his way to competency in Anglican theology, English literature, and Latin poetry, and was otherwise fulfilling his father's provincial dream of having a perfect English gentleman for a son.

As a lawyer, William Samuel Johnson spoke out against the Stamp Act. Yet as a dutiful Anglophile he contemplated no violent measures of opposition, and fully conceded Parliament's authority over America. In 1776 he refused to take the required oath of allegiance to the free and independent state of Connecticut. Revolutionary authorities thereupon forced him to abandon his legal career and retire to his home in Stratford. Enforced inactivity and loss of income eventually caused him to change his mind. After taking the oath of allegiance in 1779, he resumed his law practice.[8]

ISRAEL PEMBERTON was a Philadelphia Quaker. Most of the leaders of this powerful and distinctive group were unsympathetic to the revolutionary movement, and many of them made no secret of their support of the British presence in America. During the war they were politically, economically, and in some cases physically abused for their ideas.

As parents, the Philadelphia Quakers were known for their strictness with their children. Yet instead of resenting the fact that they were being raised in a sterner fashion than their non-Quaker contemporaries, the children seemed to welcome the discipline.

Israel Pemberton was born in 1715, the son of Israel Pemberton, Sr., a prominent Philadelphia merchant and one of the best-known leaders of the Society of Friends in his generation. During the 1730s and 1740s he also served in the Pennsylvania legislature. In the opinion of his son's biographer, the senior Pemberton adhered as closely to the Quaker philosophy as was humanly possible. His wife likewise lived strictly by the teachings of the Friends. Not surprisingly, they sent their son to a Friends school, so that his education would reinforce the training he received at home.

Young Israel unquestioningly accepted his parents' religious ideas and way of life. When it came time for the boy to decide on a career, the choice was automatic. He became a merchant, as his father had.

Throughout his adulthood, the younger Israel Pemberton was known for his unshakable convictions, strong will, and capacity to lead. Just as he had never doubted his parents' wisdom, so he never doubted his own righteousness. The "King of the Quakers," people called him. In 1776, "King" Pemberton looked upon George III through the authoritarian perspective of a lifetime, and found no reason to renounce him.[9]

SAMUEL SEABURY "was his father's son," says one of his biographers, "in physical appearance, as well as in the cast of his mind." His father's influence, indeed, was "clearly decisive in molding his character." Another biographer has similarly affirmed that "Samuel Seabury, the father, was a very important influence in the life of his son, the Bishop, because of the unusually close relationship between them."

The senior Samuel Seabury began his career in the ministry as a Congregational preacher at North Yarmouth on the Maine frontier. About the time of his namesake's birth in 1729, he became convinced that hierarchical forms gave an order and meaning to life, and that an episcopacy was essential to the effective operation of a Christian church. His switch to Episcopalianism was also a means of ingratiating himself with his father-in-law. For Thomas Mumford, a well-to-do merchant and farmer in Connecticut, was an Episcopal convert and an enthusiastic proselytizer for the faith. He eventually gave a substantial amount of money for the construction of a fine new church in New London, to which his son-in-law, by no accident, was appointed minister.

During the religious awakening of the 1730s and 1740s, New London was the scene of wild disorders, which made life very difficult for the personally diffident, philosophically conservative Reverend Mr. Seabury. When, for example, the revivalist Gilbert Tennent came to New London for two days of preaching in 1741, his hellfire sermons ignited an emotional blaze that raged uncontrollably for weeks. In order to calm the terrified citizens and bring them back from "their amazing apprehensions" of eternal damnation to a "Just notion of the Doctrine of Repentance and the Remission of Sins," Seabury first had to overcome his own fear of mob emotion. Since there were no other Episcopal ministers in town to lend him comfort and support, he walked among the people in the company of his twelve-year-old son, Samuel. Watching his father as he tried to soothe the crowd with his "plain expositions of the Terms of Reconciliation with God," young Sam came to the conclusion that he, too, would fight "Enthusiasm" when he grew up.

Not long after the emotional orgy let loose by Gilbert Tennent, the senior Seabury left New London to become the rector of Hempstead parish on Long Island. With only fifty-six communicants in his New London church, he had clearly not been the victor in the battle against enthusiasm. Yet the change of scene made him no happier. Like other puritanical New Englanders before and after him, he found New Yorkers to be disconcertingly uninterested in the serious business of life. The provincial government, he complained, did nothing to encourage religion, while political appointments were made on the basis of party affiliation rather than the state of the candidate's soul. "Profaneness," he said, "meets with no frown from the Civil Magistrate." Even amongst his neighbors in Hempstead, he missed having friends who were as strictly religious as he was.

In his loneliness he once again turned to the "solid, sensible, virtuous youth" who was his namesake. After completing his schooling under his father's direction, young Sam had crossed Long Island Sound and entered Yale, but his father's appeal for help brought him scurrying home again. The return symbolized a submission of the son to the father that would last until the latter's death from a nervous disorder in 1764.

When young Sam went to Scotland in the late 1740s to study medicine, it was his father who decided that he should do so ("I intend, God willing that he shall spend one or two years at Edinburgh in the study of Physic," the senior Seabury wrote to a friend), even as it was his father who had previously selected Sam out of his large brood of children to follow him into the ministry. Samuel Seabury, Jr., served for four years at a church in Huntington, Long Island, and in 1757 accepted the rectorship of Grace Church in Jamaica, Long Island, because both appointments brought him close to a beleaguered father who could not bear to live without his son, and whose direction the dutiful son counted on in everything he did. Not until 1766 did Samuel Seabury, no longer Junior, leave Long Island for a new post elsewhere.[10]

JONATHAN SEWALL, born in 1728, was the descendant of generations of Massachusetts judges, militia officers, and legislators. Stephen Sewall, for example, Jonathan's grandfather, was a political leader and militia officer in Salem. The father of several sons, Stephen Sewall raised his boys in the expectation that they would also become prominent members of the community. All but one of his sons gladdened his heart. The exception was Jonathan, who was a financial as well as a political failure. Jonathan even had difficulty in perpetuating the family name. His first wife died childless. His second wife, whom he married in 1724, bore him six children, but only two survived, a daughter called Jane and a son who was named for his father. Three years after his son's birth, feckless Jonathan Sewall died, leaving behind him an estate made up largely of debts.

Young Jonathan thus inherited the expectations of the Sewalls, but not their traditionally advantageous position. Relatives and friends had to see to it that the boy was properly educated. The funds for his early schooling were raised among wealthy parishioners by the minister of the church that the Sewalls had attended. When it came time for him to attend Harvard, a number of highly successful relatives—who seemed otherwise uninterested in Jonathan—agreed to foot the bills.

"If he had not yet recognized the tenuous nature of his social position in Massachusetts society," Sewall's biographer Carol Berkin has written, "Harvard itself was certain to force his awareness." An institution which prided itself on its elitist traditions, Harvard publicly ranked each member of the entering class on the basis of his family's standing in the province. The question of Jonathan Sewall's ranking was complicated. On the one hand, this fatherless fifteen-year-old had no credentials to speak of. On the other hand, he was the nephew of the great Judge Sewall. The authorities finally decided to rank him eleventh out of twenty-four.

His immediate response to the tenuousness of his situation was to become a ringleader of undergraduate rebellions. In his first two years he was repeatedly in trouble for creating disturbances. For no apparent reason he seemed particularly bent on embarrassing his tutor. Finally one evening he threw a brick through the tutor's window, and found himself in serious trouble. Although the tutor was a sensitive man, he failed to realize that Sewall's assault on an authority figure was a self-destructive and despairing act; all that Mr. Joseph

Mayhew comprehended was that an undergraduate had committed an unpardonable offense. When Mayhew first confronted the culprit, Sewall denied having thrown the brick, despite the fact that the other boys who had been with him said that he had. Infuriated by the boy's defiance, Mayhew threatened to bring a civil action unless he admitted his guilt. Sewall thereupon confessed. Mayhew thereupon had him expelled.

For two years, Sewall taught school in nearby Watertown, hoping and praying for reinstatement. His applications were consistently turned down, however. Through these repeated rejections, says Carol Berkin, Sewall learned the high price of rebellion. Finally in 1751, four years after his college class had been graduated, Sewall was readmitted, but on humiliating terms which again reminded him of the consequences of flouting authority. Instead of allowing him to come back quietly, the college insisted that he make public apologies to the faculty and the students.

After finishing at Harvard, Sewall took up schoolteaching again, this time in Salem. But in 1756 he succeeded in apprenticing himself to a Middlesex County lawyer named Chambers Russell, who soon became fond of his apprentice and took him into his home and supported him. Russell was everything that young Sewall's own father had not been. He was a vice-admiralty judge and a justice of the Massachusetts Superior Court. The political leader of his county, he served for twenty-six years in the General Court. While acquiring political power, he had also accumulated an impressive fortune. Conflicting feelings about authority figures had once caused Sewall to play a destructive prank on his tutor. Sewall's expulsion from Harvard, however, had permanently inhibited him from giving expression to his antiauthoritarian resentments. At age twenty-eight, he was prepared, nay, eager, to make Chambers Russell's every wish Jonathan Sewall's command.

Carol Berkin makes the point that in addition to viewing Russell as his surrogate father, Sewall also saw in Russell's relationship with the Middlesex County constituency that he virtually governed "all the admirable qualities of the father-child relationship." The old judge was the paternal protector of the community, as Sewall interpreted the situation, and the community responded with the deference of grateful children. It was a perfect arrangement. In the eulogy he wrote at the time of Russell's death, Sewall made the father-child analogy the centerpiece of his political praise. Thereafter, Sewall lived by the conviction that "the paternal care of the majority by a privileged but responsibility-laden minority was rational, necessary, and productive of social harmony." He also lived by the personal conviction that the sponsorship of powerful, older men was absolutely essential to his career. With the passing of Chambers Russell, Sewall turned to Governor Bernard and other men in the inner circle of Massachusetts government, who were in a position to do him favors in exchange for his devoted services to them.

As Russell had, his new sponsors encouraged him to rise above his terrible nervousness about public speaking. (Did the problem stem from the time that he had been compelled to apologize to Harvard?) Soon he developed into the most accomplished courtroom lawyer in Boston. John Adams spoke of his "soft, smooth, insinuating eloquence, which glided imperceptibly into the minds of a jury." His powerful friends also helped him to become a judge of admiralty, like Chambers Russell, as well as advocate general, solicitor general, and attorney general of Massachusetts.

Privately, Sewall was appalled by the provocative behavior of British customs officers, and he advised John Adams to make his reputation by opposing imperial policies. But he himself would not take such a risk. The faintly ironic manner he developed was the only public sign of the subversive feelings he still harbored.

In the aftermath of the Boston Massacre, Sewall's cool self-control began to crack. By the beginning of 1775 he was a depressed and frightened man, and when fighting erupted in

April, he fled to England with the advance guard of Tory exiles. In an effort to expunge his American nightmares, he changed the spelling of his name to Sewell, claiming that only immigrants to the New World spelled it Sewall. But such strategies could not repair the psychic damage he had been dealt. The destruction of his public career had destroyed the inner man as well. In 1785 he suffered a mental breakdown from which he never fully recovered. Insisting to the end that oligarchy was the best form of government among men, he died in 1796.[11]

WILLIAM SMITH of New York was forced to make a decision on July 4, 1776, which he dearly would have liked to avoid. Other Americans experienced difficulty in making up their minds that summer, but Smith's dilemma was exceptionally painful. In earlier years, after all, he had worked against the extension of Parliamentary power over the colonies in matters of taxation, and had been an outspoken opponent of the Stamp Act. The Sons of Liberty had courted his support in 1774, under the impression that he was a radical. After he suggested the oppositionist policy which led to the calling of the first Continental Congress, it was generally agreed that the lawyer from New York was a good man in a crisis. Yet Smith was politically more troubled than he seemed. When his fellow Whigs began to speak seriously of independence, Smith became even more upset. Such talk was ruinous, he said; it was evil; he would not listen to it. No one in his right mind would wish to leave the empire. Even after the Declaration of Independence was proclaimed, he could not believe that separation was actively desired by more than a small minority of the colonists. As for himself, he refused to be pressured into swearing an oath of Revolutionary allegiance. With the denunciations of erstwhile friends ringing in his ears, he went off to a lonely exile in upcountry New York.

His biographer, Leslie F. S. Upton, ascribes Smith's decision to his legal training, which had endowed him with a profound respect for the British government and its traditions. Further-more, says Upton, Smith's successful law practice had made him one of the wealthiest men in the province of New York, with a vested interest in preserving society as it was. Yet even if it could be demonstrated—which it cannot be—that wealthy lawyers were generally pro-British, the temperamental origins of Smith's loyalism would still need to be acknowledged. The introspective, indecisive son of a tremendously vigorous and self-assured father, Smith never outgrew his awe of paternal authority. Beneath all his vacillations—his "contrapuntal tendencies," as Michael Kammen calls them—lay an unwaver-ing belief that in unity there was strength. Personally this meant that he always worked in tandem with his father. Po-litically it meant that he ardently supported cooperation be-tween colonial America and imperial Britain. He denounced the Stamp Act because it was divisive, and he opposed the Declaration of Independence for the same reason. In William Smith's daunted vision of life, it was unsafe to stand alone.

William Smith, Sr., the father of the loyalist, was born in England, but came to America in 1715, was graduated from Yale in 1719, took an M.A. in 1722, and stayed on as a tutor at the college until 1724. At the age of twenty-seven he was offered the Yale presidency, but turned it down, just as he had earlier shrugged off his family's hopes that he would en-ter the Presbyterian ministry. Smith wanted a legal career, and he allowed nothing to swerve him from his iron way. His rise in his chosen profession was spectacularly swift. While still a young man, he was recognized as a pillar of the New York bar, and in the 1740s and 1750s was the foremost teacher of law in the province of New York. In 1754 he became a dele-gate to the Albany Congress. In 1763 he was appointed to a judgeship on the New York Supreme Court. For fourteen years he served as a member of the Council. He helped to found the first English Presbyterian Church in New York, and was a prominent member of the so-called Presbyterian faction in provincial politics. In the younger William Smith's *History of the Province of New-York,* the author saluted his father as a great man. The senior Smith was a master, said his son, of the arts of persuasion, for "he had the natural advantages of figure, voice, vivacity, memory, imagination, promptness, strong passions, volubility, invention, and a taste for ornament." He was assiduously industrious, his son continued; he had a robust constitution; he was temperate in his habits; he knew science as well as law and theology; in short, he was a paragon of paragons.

William Smith, Jr., born in 1728, tried hard to follow in his father's giant footsteps. He, too, went to Yale, and immediately after college entered his father's law office. Thanks to his father's influence, he was commissioned to edit the laws of the province of New York from 1691 to the present. Throughout his legal career he carried on his father's campaign to raise the standards of jurisdiction in small causes. He became as prominent a teacher of law in the 1760s and 1770s as his father had been in the preceding two decades. He allied himself with his father's political faction. He attended the Albany Congress in his father's company. He maintained a country house in Haverstraw, New York, where his father had a summer retreat. In 1760, the elder Smith haughtily turned down the Chief Justiceship of the Supreme Court because he could not have it with life tenure. Three years later his son rejected a similar invitation. When his father retired from the Council in 1767, his son took his seat.

Yet as Michael Kammen has pointed out, William Smith, Jr., did not really have the appetite for the hurly-burly of politics and the law that his father did. He sought a public career because his father had. But in trying to become someone he was not, he failed to become a man in his own right. Sensitive, bookish, but agonizingly irresolute, the younger Smith began to dream in his adolescent years of escaping completely from the world of affairs—at the same time that he was feverishly aping his father's worldly involvement. In 1744, at the age of sixteen, he wrote an essay on "retirement," and two years later imagined himself living a life of contemplation in "a solitary Hermetical retreat." In 1750, the year in which he received his license to practice law, he confessed that the routine of a law office "imbitters my life in every part of it." Nevertheless he pursued the law, while his literary interests remained a kind of hobby. By the time his father died in 1769, it was too late for him to wipe the slate clean and begin his career all over again. Ironically, it was only when Revolutionary officials forced him into rural exile that his fantasy of "retirement" became a full-scale reality.[12]

BENJAMIN THOMPSON, in his European years, was renowned for his contributions to physics, his numerous technological innovations, and his generous philanthropies. In his native Woburn, Massachusetts, however, he was remembered as a traitor to the Revolution.

He was born in 1753 and named for his father. Unfortunately, the senior Thompson died when his son was two years old. A year later his mother married Josiah Pierce, who proved to be a harsh and unsympathetic stepfather. The tension between Benjamin and Pierce was further increased by the boy's dislike of the work that Pierce ordered him to do on the family farm.

After finishing grammar school, Benjamin took a job as a clerk in a store, but did not like the work any more than he had liked farming. In the course of the next four years he drifted into and out of a number of other low-paying jobs, including schoolkeeping, which he also disliked. At seventeen, he was a disoriented, thoroughly frustrated young man. His daydreams of becoming a doctor some day were mocked by the drab reality of his life. Then in rapid succession he ingratiated himself with a series of important men, who not only transformed his social and economic situation, but filled his psychic need to pay homage to wealth and power.

The first of these men was the Reverend Timothy Walker, a well-connected and well-to-do clergyman in Concord, New Hampshire. Under Walker's supervision, Thompson became a reasonable facsimile of a young gentleman. Soon he was being encouraged to court Walker's daughter, even though his motives for doing so must have been obvious to everyone. For the daughter was a widow who would never see thirty again, and whose principal attractions were her imposing home and large income. At nineteen, Thompson married her. Shortly before the ceremony, the Reverend Mr. Walker sent the youth off to Boston to buy a hussar's coat with mock-spangle buttons, so that he would be sure to cut a gallant figure at the wedding.

In the year of his marriage, Thompson also managed to attach himself to Governor John Wentworth. Attracted as the Reverend Mr. Walker had been by the youth's intelligence and eagerness to please, Wentworth offered him a commission as a major in the militia. Not yet twenty years old, the ex-store clerk from Woburn now stepped before the world as Major Thompson, the wealthy New Hampshire squire. The year was 1772.

"From principle I supported the King," Thompson later said, but in fact he was motivated by unappeased ambition, not by principle. He was attracted to Toryism because his benefactor of the moment, Governor Wentworth, was a Tory, and because the other authority figures who happened to catch his eye were also devotees of George III. The young officer kept his thoughts to himself, however, with the result that many patriots were deceived into thinking that he was one of them. Not until it was too late did they discover that he had acted as a secret informer for General Gage.

After escaping to London in 1776, Thompson was taken under the wing of yet another influential official, Lord George Germain, the secretary for the colonies, who found a government sinecure for him. Moving on to the Continent, Thompson cultivated close relationships with a number of noblemen, including the Elector of Bavaria, who in gratitude for many services dubbed him Count Rumford of the Holy Roman Empire.[13]

PETER VAN SCHAACK was the youngest of seven children of a merchant in Kinderhook, New York. Although uneducated, the merchant had a powerful intelligence, which was reinforced by an inflexible will. According to his son's nineteenth-century biographer, the sense of personal force communicated by this domineering Dutchman filled people with awe. As a parent, the elder Van Schaack had no interest in making compromises with his children. Young Peter, for example, wanted very much to enter the army, but his father waved aside the idea. He had "designed" his son to be a lawyer or a minister, and that was that.

In school, Peter encountered an equally rigid discipline. His teacher's impatient manner, violent temper, and fanatical insistence that Peter answer all questions addressed to him caused the boy to become "possessed of an idea that my talents were defective, and that I was not designed by nature to pursue the paths of science." He therefore approached his father once again, and pleaded with him "to permit me to leave my books, and to indulge me in my wishes of going into the army." But as before, his father was "utterly averse" to the idea. Shortly thereafter, Peter was dispatched to Staten Island, where an Episcopal clergyman offered him "rigid instruction" in Latin. In the early 1760s the youth studied at King's College in New York, then took up law, exactly as his father had wished.

A decade later, Peter Van Schaack opposed independence, because, he said, without a "controlling common umpire, the colonies must become independent states, which would be introductive of anarchy and confusion among ourselves."[14]

A number of the loyalists whose backgrounds have been described in this chapter were raised by stern and uncompromising patriarchs who tolerated no questioning of their dictatorship of family affairs. In such households, the notion that children had a right to their own opinions about what was best for them was regarded as akin to sacrilege. Other loyalists, by contrast, suffered from a lack of paternal guidance in their formative years, owing to the demoralization or the early death of their fathers; haunted by feelings of insecurity, these men never outgrew their childish desires to be admired and protected by powerful authority figures. Still other loyalists, most conspicuously Thomas Hutchinson, were raised by fathers who wanted to hold on to their children after they were grown up, and who consequently did not prepare them to exchange the familiar routines of home for the strangeness and uncertainty of independence. William Franklin's unhealthy sense of inferiority to Benjamin was the archetype of yet another sort of relationship between a loyalist son and his father.

While the evidence I have assembled here is too slim to support convincing generalizations about the childhoods of all the men who opposed the American Revolution, it is also true that in the loyalist biographies that contain meaningful descriptions of father-son relationships I did not find a single exception to the sorts of relationships I have summarized above. Information on the family backgrounds of the loyalists is woefully incomplete, but so far as I have been able to determine it is not contradictory. The possibility exists, then, that loyalist Americans were bound together as a group by certain kinds of childhood experience, and that they opposed the American Revolution for reasons that were related by an emotional logic to the way they had been brought up. The lives of the men described in this chapter may not sustain conclusions, but they raise fascinating questions.

Notes

1. Wallace Brown, *The Good Americans. The Loyalists in the American Revolution* (New York, 1969), pp. 2-29.

2. Willard M. Wallace, *Traitorous Hero. The Life and Fortunes of Benedict Arnold* (New York, 1954), pp. 3-198.

3. Jonathan Boucher, *Reminiscences of an American Loyalist,* ed. Jonathan Bouchier (Boston, 1925), *passim.* Jonathan Boucher, *A View of the Causes and Consequences of the American Revolution* (London, 1797), pp. 528-29, 530 n., 592. Michael D. Clark, "Jonathan Boucher: The Mirror of Reaction," *The Huntington Library Quarterly,* XXXIII, 1 (November, 1969), pp. 19-32. "Letters of Rev. Jonathan Boucher," *Maryland Historical Magazine,* VII, 1 (March, 1912), pp. 1-26. "Letters of Rev. Jonathan Boucher," *Maryland Historical Magazine,* VII, 3 (September, 1912), pp. 286-303. Ralph Emmett Fall, "The Rev. Jonathan Boucher, Turbulent Tory (1738-1804)," *Historical Magazine of the Protestant Episcopal Church,* XXXVI, 4 (December, 1967), pp. 323-58. Robert McCluer Calhoon, *The Loyalists in Revolutionary America,* 1760-1781 (New York, 1973), pp. 220-24.

4. Arthur Wentworth Hamilton Eaton, *The Famous Mather Byles* (Freeport, New York, 1971), pp. 15-77. [Originally published 1914.] Cotton Mather, *Bonifacius. An Essay Upon the Good,* ed. David Levin (Cambridge, Mass., 1966), pp. 42-52.

5. Calhoon, p. 136. Aubrey C. Land, *The Dulanys of Maryland* (Baltimore, 1968), pp. 4-265. [Originally published 1955.]

6. Catherine Fennelly, "William Franklin of New Jersey," *The William and Mary Quarterly,* 3rd ser., VI, 3 (July, 1949), pp. 361-82. Carl Van Doren, *Benjamin Franklin* (New York, 1961), pp. 200-01, 231, 480. [Originally published 1938.] Brown, p. 66. Calhoon, pp. 120-21, 125.

7. Bernard Bailyn, *The Ordeal of Thomas Hutchinson* (Cambridge, Mass., 1974), pp. 10-31, 35, 139, 331-80.

8. George C. Groce, Jr., *William Samuel Johnson. A Maker of the Constitution* (New York, 1937), pp. 3-111.

9. Theodore Thayer, *Israel Pemberton. King of the Quakers* (Philadelphia, 1943), pp. iii, 4, 5, 15.

10. Herbert Thoms, *Samuel Seabury, Priest and Physician. Bishop of Connecticut* (Hamden, Conn., 1963), pp. 15-41. Bruce E. Steiner, *Samuel Seabury, 1729-1796. A Study in the High Church Tradition* (Athens, Ohio, 1971), pp. 5-79.

11. Carol Berkin, *Jonathan Sewall, Odyssey of an American*

Loyalist (New York, 1974), pp. 1-161. Calhoon, pp. 68-74.

12. Leslie F. S. Upton, "William Smith, Chief Justice of New York and Quebec, 1728-1793," Ph.D. diss., University of Minnesota, 1957), pp. 2-180. William Smith, Jr., *The History of the Province of New-York*, 2 vols., ed. Michael Kammen (Cambridge, Mass., 1972), I, pp. xvii-xxi; II, p. 34.

13. W. J. Sparrow, *Knight of the White Eagle* (London, 1964), 17-43.

14. Henry C. Van Schaack, *The Life of Peter Van Schaack, LL.D.* (New York, 1842), pp. 1-57.

CHAPTER TWO

Patriot Backgrounds

JOHN ADAMS was born in Braintree, Massachusetts, in 1735, the son of a farmer and maltster. His mother, Susanna Boylston Adams, was the daughter of one of the most prominent families in Boston. A man of driving energy, the maltster not only worked at two occupations and raised three sons, but served as a lieutenant in the local militia, a deacon of the church, and a town selectman. As his namesake wrote of him at the time of his death, John Adams, Sr., had managed most of the business of the community for twenty years. Young John also said that his father was "the honestest man I ever knew," and that "in wisdom, piety, benevolence and charity in proportion to . . . education and sphere of life, I have never seen his superior."

The encomium testified to the nature of the relationship between father and son. In the words of Page Smith, an Adams biographer, "the father's influence on the son was strong and enduring. The boy loved and admired him, and sought, in all things, to imitate him." Young John also seems to have been quite attached to his mother, although it is not entirely clear what he thought of her "inexhaustible stock of improving precepts."

Under his father's instruction, young John quickly learned to read, thus giving promise of being a good scholar; but when he was sent to school the child suddenly developed a resistance to education. For the schools of the area were old-

style Puritan institutions, which placed a premium on unquestioning obedience, whereas Adams had been used to the
milder authority of his father. Shortly after completing pri-
mary instruction and enrolling in a Latin school, he fell into
the habit of skipping classes. A good hunter, he loved to roam
the Blue Hills, looking for wild life. He was also very fond of
competitive sports—they suited his fiercely aggressive, not to
say violent nature—and he became especially adept at wrest-
ling, in spite of the fact that most of his contemporaries were
taller and heavier than he was.

Eventually his father became somewhat alarmed by his
son's lack of interest in school. "What would you be, child?"
he asked him one day. To which young John replied that he
wanted to be a farmer, like his father. The senior Adams immediately took him off for a day of work in a muddy bottom,
cutting and binding cumbersome bundles of thatch. That
night, the boy's back and arm muscles were sore to the touch,
but when his father asked him what he now thought of farming, he declared that he still liked it. His father shot back that
his own opinion of the occupation was much lower—"so you
shall go to school." Back in the classroom again, young Adams
sought to fend off boredom by asking the master's permission to proceed at a faster pace in mathematics than the rest
of his schoolmates. The permission was granted, and he quickly finished the course without the assistance of the teacher.
But the pleasure he took in this achievement was more than
offset by the pain of studying Latin. The language was unin-
teresting, and the teacher an intolerable bore. Unable to force
himself to pay attention in class, Adams began to develop
guilt feelings about going against his father's wishes. Finally
he confronted his father and again asked to be removed from
school and put to work on the family farm. "You know I have
set my heart on your education at college. Why must you
resist?" his father asked. Responding to his parent's obvious
disappointment, Young John altered his request. "Sir," he

said, "I don't like my schoolmaster. He is so negligent and so cross that I never can learn anything under him. If you will be so good as to persuade Mr. Marsh to take me [Joseph Marsh was the son of a former minister in Braintree, and both Adamses knew him to be an able Latin scholar as well as an attractive person], I will apply myself to my studies as closely as my nature will admit and go to college as soon as I can be prepared." After conferring with Marsh, Adams's father agreed to his son's proposal and the matter was settled.

What is most striking about this episode is the respect that father and son exhibit for one another at every point of their disagreement. The father will have the final say, of course, and both of them know it, but there is no disposition on the senior Adams' part to break his son's will. Instead of laying down the law in an unreasoning and tyrannical manner, he takes his son to the farm in order to persuade him of the wisdom of remaining in school. Only when experience fails to open his son's eyes to the limitations of a farmer's life does the father become insistent. And when his son comes to him a second time to complain about conditions at school, he is again willing to listen to his protest and ultimately accepts his compromise solution. The thirteen-year-old boy had been held to an educational ideal, but not at the cost of his spirit. Given young John's impulsiveness and combativeness, a more inflexible father might have caused the boy to run away. Instead, he remained under his parents' roof, submitted to the instruction of the patient, kindly Marsh—and promptly discovered that he not only had a huge capacity for intellectual work, but a genuine passion for it. At age fifteen a burningly ambitious youth left home and entered Harvard.

His childhood, which was now over, had left Adams with an exhilarating sense of his own powers. But it had also taught him something about the interaction between two spheres of interest, and about how useful it was to have them limit one another. This lesson stayed with him, through the colonial resistance to British authority—which Adams came to despise for its unwillingness to compromise—and beyond. His recommendation that the mixed-government principle be embodied in the constitutions of all the states in the American Union reflected a great many experiences in his mature life, including his reading of Montesquieu. But it also reflected his experience of growing up. [1]

SAM ADAMS was the son of a well-to-do brewer and merchant in Boston who was also a devout member of the Congregational Church. Deacon Adams, as he was called, very much wanted his namesake to have a career in the ministry. When the boy entered Harvard with the class of 1740, it was with the expectation that he would fulfill his father's ambition for him. Almost immediately, however, the fourteen-year-old Sam made it clear that he had no interest in studying theology. Instead of pressing his son, the elder Adams quietly abandoned his long-held dream of seeing him in a pulpit. The boy's own preference was for the law, mainly because of the vivid interest in politics he shared with his father. In the course of his career, the elder Adams served as one of the Boston representatives in the General Court, helped to organize the Boston Caucus, and was an energetic spokesman for colonial rights. Unfortunately, his wife was opposed to the idea of a legal career for their son, possibly because she thought it to be beneath the dignity of the family.

With the blessing of both parents, the young Harvard graduate finally entered Thomas Cushing's counting house; if he could not be a lawyer, he would become a wealthy merchant. It took only a few months for everyone to discover that he was not paying attention to business. He then left the house of Cushing, and with a loan of a thousand pounds from his father—who was beginning to worry about his son—made plans to go into business for himself. The plans did not work out, though, because Sam lent some of the money to a friend, who promptly squandered it. While the elder Adams was undoubtedly angered by his son's prodigality, he did not quarrel with the now-evident fact that his namesake had no more aptitude for business than he had for the ministry. In his will, old Sam provided that his son not be required to repay the loan. So that young Sam would have a livelihood, his father also offered him a position in his own brewing business, but refrained from filling his days so full of beer, rum, and molasses that he did not have time for his real love, which was politics. In 1748, the year of the elder Adams' death, Sam finished the first of his important political diatribes, in which he denounced the materialism of modern life and called for a return to simpler ways. On his own terms, he had in fact become a preacher, as his father had wished. Another seventeen years would pass, however, before the Sugar Act and the Stamp Act finally gave this brilliant propagandist his great chance. Thanks to his father's concern that he be allowed to lead the life he wanted to, he was able to bide his time, perfect his polemical techniques, and seize his opportunity when it finally arrived.[2]

CHARLES CARROLL of Carrollton came home to Maryland in 1765, after seventeen years of absence from his family. He was twenty-eight years old.

The problem was that the Carrolls were Catholic. Schools in the American colonies were regulated by codes which in effect required Catholic children to give up their faith before matriculating. Employing Catholic tutors in private homes was also forbidden. Enrolling one's children in English Catholic colleges on the Continent was equally unlawful. Inasmuch as the last regulation was the easiest to violate, families which had money, as the Carrolls most certainly did, generally arranged to have their children educated abroad. Charles Carroll,

Sr., had himself studied in Europe as a boy. It was a natural decision, then, that he should send off his son and namesake to a Jesuit college in France when he reached the age of eleven. A natural decision, but not an easy one. The Carrolls were a close-knit family, and the parents found it an emotionally difficult task to prepare their son for a long separation from them. Nevertheless they carried through with it.

In a flood of letters, the Carrolls kept in close touch with young Charles during his long sojourn abroad. Throughout his boyhood they fulfilled their parental responsibilities by giving him detailed advice about what to do and how to behave. Yet they were wise enough to refrain from interfering with his life to the point where they might have endangered his ability to fend for himself in an alien environment. Their concern was constant, but never tyrannical or even condescending. A letter from Charles, Sr., to his son in 1756, a week after the latter's nineteenth birthday, is typical. It begins with a recommendation that young Charles learn to fence under a good master, for "a gentleman should know how to defend himself when attacked." The elder Carroll then goes on to say that

> Your mother is very desirous of having your picture, and I hope you will gratify her if you can find a good limner; let the size of the picture be about fifteen inches long and ten inches wide. You had good hair when a child; if it continues so, pray wear it; it will become you better than a wig, and beside you will be more in the fashion. I presume you will have all the letters I have wrote to you by you; it may not be improper now and then to overlook them; I never wrote to you as a child, and therefore you may reap some advantage from a serious perusal of them. My dear child, I wish you success in your studies, and a daily increase of God's grace and blessings on you.

The basic assumption of this rather Chesterfieldian letter is that the father is wise in the ways of the world, and that his inexperienced son will benefit from his wisdom; this is why the son has undoubtedly kept all the letters he has ever received from his father, and why he would benefit from rereading them at this time. There is also another reason why he might profitably pick them up again: "I never wrote to you as a child." The advice from America to Europe has not flowed *de haut en bas*, and therefore Charles Carroll at nineteen will not find letters addressed to an eleven-year-old beneath his dignity.

A letter from mother to son in the same period says in part, "Your papa's love for you is so great, and he is so well pleased with your diligence, improvement, and good dispositions, that he is inclined to do everything for your satisfaction and advantage. . . ." This was a fair statement of her husband's parental philosophy. A man of great wealth, Charles Carroll, Sr., had the financial means to make a broad range of experience available to an innocent abroad, and he did not hesitate to do so. If he counseled his son to pick his intimates with care, he also urged him to seek the company of a wide variety of men and women, to spend his money on travel and the acquisition of new skills, and to enjoy himself. Be "cheerful, lively, easy and polite," he urged young Charles.

Having always been treated in a man-to-man fashion by his absent father, young Charles Carroll eventually developed a prophetic sense that the thirteen colonies would not consent to being treated as little children by an arbitrary authority on the other side of the Atlantic Ocean. In 1763, at the outset of the new and stricter phase of British interference in American affairs, he wrote a letter to his father from London and told him of the feeling he had. "America is a growing country; in time it will and must be independent."[3]

BENJAMIN FRANKLIN remembered thirteen at table when he was growing up in Boston in the first and second decades of the new century. His father, Josiah, had seven children by his first wife and ten by his second. Ben's mother was swamped with domestic duties and seems not to have given much time to her most gifted child. In any event, the child rarely mentioned her in later years. His father, on the other hand, was important to him. This maker and seller of soap and candles was "seasoned and shrewd," in Carl Van Doren's words, "orthodox but not too devout," and "cheerful among his houseful of children." He taught two of his sons, John and Peter, the chandler's trade, and might have taught his namesake as well, except that young Josiah ran away to sea and was later lost. Yet the senior Franklin had no wish to force all his sons into the same mold. James's desire to be a printer received his blessing, and he encouraged bright little Ben to aim for a professional career. To that end, he sent him to grammar school at the age of eight. Perhaps he would become a minister.

Mounting household bills soon forced old Josiah to realize that he would never be able to send Ben to college. He therefore withdrew him from the grammar school at the end of a year and enrolled him in a more modest institution, which taught writing and arithmetic. Possibly because of his disappointment at having to leave the grammar school, Ben quickly contrived to fail in arithmetic. At age ten he was removed from the school and taken home to assist his father in business.

During the next two years Josiah was his teacher. But while father and son got along well enough, Ben was unhappy. He disliked tallow, and dreamed of washing his hands of it in the sea. He would become a sailor, as his brother Josiah had. Spurred by the fear of losing another son, the senior Franklin undertook to find a job for him in Boston that appealed to his imagination and suited his talents. Together, father and son made a tour of local craftsmen, talking to joiners, bricklayers, and braziers. Finally, the bookishness of the boy inspired Josiah to apprentice him to a printer, who happened to be Ben's twenty-one-year-old brother James. Although Ben still yearned for the life of a sailor, he clearly preferred printing to soap making, and therefore agreed to a compromise solution that he could not have avoided except by running away. Once again, the father of a future patriot had demonstrated flexibility rather than an unreasoning tyranny. For his part, Ben had displayed the sort of conciliatory spirit that later would become the hallmark of his diplomacy.

Ben worked for James from the time he was twelve until he left Boston five years later. In this period old Josiah sometimes offered Ben advice about his prose style which the budding writer found useful, as well as "frequent counsel" about the necessity of being an industrious, honest, and prudent apprentice. When the brothers quarreled, as they frequently did, they again came to their father, who usually came down on his younger son's side of the argument.

Nevertheless Ben was legally bound to James, and "the father, for all his care, had yielded most of his authority to the elder brother," as Carl Van Doren's biography makes clear. The trouble was that James was a tyrant and Ben was an unwilling slave. In his frustration James began to beat his upstart apprentice, especially after it dawned on him that Ben had more literary talent than he had. When James was jailed for contempt of the authorities, Ben blithely carried on the *New England Courant* by himself, even though he was only sixteen. His *Dogood Papers* also received extravagant praise. These developments caused James to discern a disgusting vanity in his apprentice. The beatings resumed. Ben had agreed to serve James until he was twenty-one, but nothing in his earlier life with his father had prepared him to accept such treatment. At age seventeen he surreptitiously slipped aboard a vessel bound for New York, and was gone.

In later years, Benjamin Franklin would devote all his diplomatic skills to maintaining British-American harmony. When, however, the lawyer Wedderburn, the future Lord Loughborough, subjected him to a humiliating interrogation at a meeting of the Council, his celebrated moderation gave way to a revolutionary temper—albeit he temporarily kept his feelings to himself. Like the runaway of old, Franklin was unwilling to forgive fundamental assaults on his dignity.[4]

NATHANAEL GREENE was commissioned a brigadier general in the Continental Army at age thirty-three. After the war he settled on an impressive plantation near Savannah, Georgia. He had come a long way from the farm in Warwick County, Rhode Island, where he had been born.

The farm was a drab and unrewarding place, requiring endless labor by Nathanael and his six brothers, as well as by Mrs. Greene, who was the farmer's second wife and anxious to please her husband. Mr. Greene, too, worked hard to improve his acreage, in addition to serving as a Quaker preacher in nearby Rhode Island communities. A sternly conservative man, he shared the view of many Quakers that the basic skills of reading, writing, and arithmetic constituted enough education for any child. More extensive training was merely an affectation. His sons belonged in the fields.

Nevertheless, says Greene's biographer Theodore Thayer, Nathanael's father was good-hearted. When Nathanael finally got up his courage and declared that he was not trying to shirk his share of the chores, but that he wanted very much to study Latin and mathematics, his father rose above his anti-intellectual prejudices and agreed to hire Adam Maxwell, a local schoolmaster, to tutor him. "The youth's powers of persuasion and compelling arguments had won. The elder Greene was not given to changing his mind readily, but he listened when Nathanael spoke." The father's decision in favor of the son was the take-off point of a meteoric rise.[5]

JOHN HANCOCK was born in 1737, the son of a minister. His father, however, died when he was seven, and the boy was adopted by his uncle, Thomas Hancock. Thomas himself was the son of a minister, which caused him to identify his foster child with his own dramatic life. Forced into the world at age thirteen by the poverty of his family, Thomas had apprenticed himself to a binder and seller of books. Seven years later he opened his own shop. The scarcity of currency sometimes caused customers to pay him in pork and cheese, which Thomas then sold at a markup. Soon he was shipping cargoes of commodities to London, to pay for the books he wished to import. In 1730 his marriage to Lydia Henchman, the daughter of the wealthiest book dealer in Boston, gave him the money and the business connections to expand his entrepreneurial schemes. He built up a papermaking business, exported codfish and whale oil, provisioned the Newfoundland fishing fleet, smuggled Dutch goods into Boston by way of the West Indies, fitted out privateers, and in 1739 secured contracts to supply the British forces fighting the French. When his fatherless nephew entered his household in 1744, Thomas Hancock was already one of the richest men in America.

Young John's doting uncle and aunt kept him out of school for a year while he became accustomed to living with them in their mansion. They were concerned, too, about the boy's health—not without cause, for he was never robust and would die at fifty-six. Even so, there was no doubt that Thomas and Lydia pampered the boy. When John Adams later complained of his friend's peevish temper, he was unwittingly calling attention to the fact that in the home of his foster parents John Hancock had not often been thwarted, and consequently became angry when he was.

After Harvard, Hancock entered his uncle's counting house. Almost at once he was given important responsibilities, such as being sent to London as Thomas' agent. But he was more than an agent; he was the heir apparent, and clients and colleagues treated him accordingly. When Thomas died without warning in 1764, John inherited a fortune of £80,000, plus the sole proprietorship of the house of Hancock. He was twenty-seven years old. For two decades, life had gone very easily for this self-willed young man, and now, just as easily, he had become rich and powerful. Was it likely that such a person would tolerate imperial interference in his business affairs in the years immediately ahead?[6]

PATRICK HENRY did not emerge from an unprivileged background, as democratic mythmakers used to insist. His father, Colonel John Henry, was the scion of comfortably middle-class Scottish parents who encouraged him to attend Kings College in Aberdeen University. But after four years at Kings, he impatiently left without a degree and took passage to Virginia in quest of fortune. He was not yet twenty years old.

Arriving in 1727, John Henry made his way into the social and political elite of Hanover County under the sponsorship of John Syme, an old friend of Henry's parents. A large landowner, a member of the House of Burgesses, and a colonel of militia, Syme was able to do a great many favors for his young protégé, of which the last and greatest was to die an untimely death in 1731, leaving behind him an attractive wife and a substantial estate. After a seemly interval, Sarah Winston Syme and John Henry were married. The ambitious young Scotsman's bride not only brought with her 6,000 acres of Hanover County land, which had belonged to her late husband, but the social prestige of her own family. Isaac Winston, her father, was a prominent merchant in the Old Dominion; her mother, Mary Dabney, had aristocratic connections on both sides of the Atlantic.

As fast as he could—for he was always in a hurry—John Henry solidified his new status. He acquired more property, hand over fist, including a one-third interest in a 30,000-acre tract in Goochland County and 1,250 acres in Albemarle County. He became the chief justice of the Hanover County Court, official surveyor of the county, a vestryman of the Church of England, and a colonel of militia. And he sired eleven children, of whom the second oldest son, born in 1736, was most like his father.

Patrick Henry and John Henry saw eye to eye, right from the start. Although both were intelligent, both had contempt for formal education as a distraction from the real business of life, which was political, social, and financial advancement. Thus the senior Henry could have afforded to send Patrick to England to be educated, but enrolled him instead in a local academy, where the boy learned to read, write, and figure. Having taken from the school what he wanted, Patrick was allowed to drop out at age ten and never required to go back. In his early teens he was tutored by his father in elementary Latin and Greek, mathematics, and ancient and modern history, so that he could pass muster as a Virginia gentleman. But the boy was much fonder of hunting than of studying, and his father saw no reason to force him to do assignments that he had no interest in. At twelve, thirteen, and fourteen, young Patrick more óften had a gun in his hands than a book. He grew toward manhood under a relaxed discipline.

At fifteen, though, he was sent off by his father to work as a clerk in a local store. While a lack of effort was permitted in the realm of book learning, John Henry had no intention of encouraging Patrick to be an idler. Shortly after he turned sixteen, Patrick and his older brother were set up by their father in a store of their own. As eager to make his fortune as John Henry had been twenty-five years earlier, Patrick welcomed these changes in his life. But events quickly revealed that he and his brother had a lot to learn about business. Within a year, their freehanded extensions of credit forced them to close the store. Yet this disillusioning experience did not demoralize Patrick, for reasons that cast light on his relationship with his father. To begin with, his father had expressed confidence, as he always had, in his son's ability. He then had backed Patrick financially, and let him alone to learn from his mistakes. When the store failed, he stood ready to back him again. Between his eighteenth and his twenty-fourth years, Patrick made a number of other occupational false starts, but they never shook his belief in his eventual success. When he finally decided to try for a legal career, he studied for a mere six weeks before being licensed to practice. Only a supreme egotist would have been willing to pit such an inadequate preparation against an examining committee consisting of Robert Carter Nicholas, John Randolph, Peyton Randolph, and George Wythe. From the moment he walked into the House of Burgesses in May 1765, Henry's political style was to strike the sun if it insulted him. What astonished the in-group of older Burgesses was the young man's utter lack of fear. When Henry introduced a series of resolutions protesting the Stamp Act, he not only recapitulated familiar formulations of the rights and privileges of all Englishmen, but argued more radically that the "General Assembly of this Colony" had "the *only* and *sole exclusive* Right and Power to lay Taxes & Impositions upon the Inhabitants of this Colony." Looking back upon this bold and defiant performance, American historians would attempt to explain it by emphasizing the western location of his home. But Patrick Henry was not the son of the frontier; he was the son of his father.[7]

JAMES MADISON did not fight in the American Revolution, but not because he was opposed to it. Physical frailty barred him from military service. Beginning in his student days at Princeton in the early 1770s, he was unqualifiedly committed to the patriots' cause.

Ambrose Madison, James's grandfather, died in 1732, leaving a thirty-six-year-old wife and three children, of whom the oldest, named James, was a boy of nine. The responsibility of running a plantation in remote and isolated Orange County, Virginia, primarily devolved upon the widow, but part of the burden fell upon her eldest child. Apparently his new duties were congenial to the boy's nature. In Irving Brant's words, "His career furnishes no evidence of rebellion from or unfitness for the domestic economy of a frontier plantation, and he was led by natural circumstances to play a leading part in the life of an isolated community." In the course of a long career, he became justice of the peace, vestryman of the church, chief of the Orange County Committee, and commander of militia, as well as master of a 5,000-acre plantation.

In 1749 he married Nelly Conway, age seventeen. James Madison, Jr., was born a little over a year later, the first of twelve children, most of whom lived to maturity. In his early years, the eldest Madison child was taught at home by his mother and grandmother. For young James, however, as for all his brothers and sisters, the dominant presence in the household and in the community at large was James Madison, Sr. "To the Madison children," says Irving Brant, "their father was always the leading figure." Powerful and tough, the senior Madison could easily have squashed the cultural ambitions of his namesake, but he did not. Even though his own intellect was restricted and his educational training slight, he was sympathetic with his first son's intellectual intensity. When the boy was eleven, he sent him to a school in King and Queen County run by Donald Robertson, a famous Virginia teacher, who taught him Latin, Greek, logic, and mathematics, in a formal sequence based on the curriculum of the first three years at the University of Edinburgh, where Robertson had once been a student. "All that I have been in life," Madison later said in a tribute to his schoolmaster, "I owe largely to that man."

After five years with Robertson, he returned to Orange County and studied for two years with a local rector before entering Princeton. James's choice of college probably surprised his father and possibly disappointed him, for Princeton was more expensive as well as more remote than William and Mary. But he did not attempt to change his son's mind. Young James decided for himself that the gambling, horse racing, and excessive drinking at Williamsburg would be intellectually distracting, and that the support given by the president of William and Mary to the idea of an American Episcopate and a state-supported church made him a foe of religious liberty, in which young James believed.

At Princeton and afterward, Madison drove himself so ferociously hard that he eventually developed epileptoid hysteria. This is a functional ailment, not an organic disease, the origins of which lie buried in psychic trauma. Irving Brant refuses to speculate on what the trauma may have involved in Madison's case, even though the symptoms he displayed— hypochondria, daydreaming, sense of physical inferiority, and compulsive overwork—all point toward his relationship with his father. Only by becoming a front-rank intellectual could a physically frail son hope to outdo the physically awesome man he was named for. Yet young James's anxieties in this regard did not alienate him from the senior Madison, or cripple his own talents. In the letters he sent home from college, James addressed his parent as "Honored Sir" and closed with "Your affectionate son." The son was still using these words in 1797, when he was forty-six and his father seventy-four. As Irving Brant says, "This lifelong habit reflected . . . a genuine respect and affection having part of its foundation in both men's strength of character." Each man was strong in his own way; each respected the strength of the other; on that basis they built an enduring relationship.[8]

JOHN MARSHALL marched off to battle against the British as a nineteen-year-old lieutenant of the Culpeper County, Virginia, minute men. The rifle on his shoulder had been lifted down from its deerhorn bracket on the wall of the Marshalls' home and placed in his hands by his father, as had the hunting knife he carried on his hip.

Thomas Marshall, the lieutenant's father, was a commandingly tall and powerful man who was further endowed, in Albert J. Beveridge's somewhat effusive phrase, with a rare intellectuality. Like Peter Jefferson, the father of Thomas

Jefferson, Thomas Marshall was a land surveyor by profession, with a reputation for never showing fatigue or fear on his treks into the Virginia wilderness. Among many other exploits, he assisted his friend George Washington in surveying the huge demesne of the Fairfaxes. In the Blue Ridge country where he eventually made his home, Thomas Marshall was far and away the most outstanding citizen. For many years he represented the area in the House of Burgesses. In the Indian wars which were a way of life on the Virginia frontier, he was repeatedly called on to serve as an officer of militia, for he was renowned for his fighting qualities, both on foot and astride a horse. Although there were many exploits he might have boasted about, Thomas Marshall was quiet and self-contained. The austerity of his manner further heightened the impressiveness of his mind and body.

Thomas and his wife Mary had fifteen children, of whom John was the eldest. For most of his childhood the boy was taught by his parents, mainly by his father. Although the Bible was the basic text, Thomas Marshall was too eager to increase his own knowledge, and too ambitious for his son, to rest content with Scriptural lessons. He encouraged John's evident delight in poetry, and probably read Shakespeare with him. But a volume of Pope was the boy's favorite book. By the time he was twelve he had copied out every word of Pope's moral essays, and had memorized great chunks of them. Under the "careful, painstaking and persistent" guidance of his father, John Marshall acquired a sense of the beauty of English literature.

Personally as well as pedagogically, the relationship between father and son was suffused, according to Beveridge's biography, with "a mutual sympathy, respect, and admiration." At the height of his later fame as a jurist, John Marshall often asserted that "my father was a far abler man than any of his sons." This was not a piety he reserved for public speeches, for the sake of inspiring young Americans of the nineteenth century to respect their parents. He also made the remark to Justice Story, when no one else was present. In his "familiar conversations with me, when there was no other listener," Story recalled, "he never named his father . . . without dwelling on his character with a fond and winning enthusiasm. . . . He broke out with a spontaneous eloquence . . . upon his virtues and talents." That the mental and physical power of Thomas Marshall generated admiration in his son, not resentment, was because the father had not used his strength to threaten the boy's integrity. The rifle and the hunting knife that Thomas Marshall placed in John Marshall's hands in the mid-1770s were symbols of manhood and freedom, not of domination and dependency.[9]

THOMAS PAINE, according to the hyperbolic John Adams, was "a mongrel between pig and puppy, begotten by a wild boar on a bitch wolf." The true facts of Paine's lineage were more ordinary. He was begotten by a corsetmaker named Joseph Pain, who earned a marginal living in Thetford, a small village seventy miles northeast of London, on a woman who was eleven years older than Pain and locally famous for her "sour temper and eccentric character." The general feeling in the village was that the main reason the mild-mannered Pain had married a shrew like Frances Cocke was because she was the daughter of an eminent attorney in Thetford and a member of the Church of England, whereas the corsetmaker came from an obscure lower-class family which worshipped with the nonconformist Society of Friends.

Both parents imposed a religious discipline upon their only child. He was brought up in the rituals of the Church of England, as his mother wished. His father made him read the Bible, and talked at length to his son about the moral necessity of personal cleanliness, including clean language. In other respects, though, the Pains were not strict. Instead of forcing young Thomas into an apprenticeship in his father's shop, they "distressed themselves" in order to give him a good education. They wanted him to rise in the world, not wait on them. Accordingly, from the time he was six to the time he was thirteen, he was sent to the village school.

Some of his studies were a liberating experience for Thomas. He discovered that "the natural bent of my mind was to science." He also enjoyed writing poetry, and fancied he had a talent for it. "A pleasing natural history of Virginia" filled his mind with enthralling images of the New World. The main business of the school, however, was to make Latinists of its graduates, and Thomas was uninterested in applying himself to "the barren study of a dead language." His "unsettled application" to his major assignments eventually disillusioned his parents. Abandoning the hope that their son would some day have a profession rather than a trade, they withdrew him from school. Joseph put him to work stitching whalebone into undergarments for the women of Thetford.

Despite his father's affectionate efforts to make the work interesting to him, Thomas found it unendurably boring. He also did not care for the lectures of his sour-tempered mother. Shortly after his sixteenth birthday he ran away from home. "Raw and adventurous, and heated with the false heroism of a master who had served in a man-of-war," he later wrote, "I began the carver of my own fortune, and entered on board the *Terrible*, privateer, Captain Death." Although his parental authority had been flouted, Joseph Pain responded with restraint. Following his boy to the docks, he did not command him, in the accents of a seventeenth-century patriarch, to come home at once. Speaking rather in the modulated voice of an eighteenth-century father, he persuaded Thomas with "affectionate and moral remonstrances" to return to Thetford. Nevertheless the ex-runaway kept close track of the *Terrible*. The ship's stunning success against the French, writes Paine's biographer David Freeman Hawke, "combined with the shrewish voice of his mother, served to undercut the power of his

father's persuasion." Thomas ran away again, and this time
Joseph felt it best to let him go. A few weeks later the youth
went to sea with the privateer *King of Prussia.*

Predictably, he did not take any more kindly to naval discipline than to his mother's tongue lashings. His father's mild
ways and forbearing disposition may have led him to expect
that male authority figures would treat him with understanding. When they insisted instead on absolute and unquestioning
obedience, he became furiously angry. How many months or
years Paine remained at sea is uncertain, but he stayed afloat
long enough, says David Freeman Hawke, "to break his ties
with home." In the back of his mind, however, he still counted
on his father as a refuge of last resort.

In 1757 Paine was listed as a journeyman corsetmaker in
London. By 1758 he was gone again. After a few more years
of knocking about southeastern England—in the course of
which time he married and buried a wife—the vagabond suddenly reappeared at his parents' home in Thetford, and was
welcomed. He spent more than a year with them, preparing
to take a qualifying examination for a position as an excise-
tax officer. Although he passed the test, he did not receive an
appointment until 1764, when he was twenty-seven years old.
Ten months later his indolence and contempt for petty regulations caused him to be dismissed.

To keep from starving, he went back to corsetmaking, first
in a village a few miles from Thetford, then in another town
somewhat further away, and finally in London. But he hated
the trade as much as ever, and could not bring himself to work
at it. Soon he was "reduced to extreme wretchedness, . . .
without food, without raiment, and without shelter." In the
fall of 1766 he talked himself into a job teaching school, although he neither liked children nor admired the salary, which
was twenty pounds a year. At some point he made a desperate
effort to earn his living as a preacher. Finally, he swallowed
his pride and wrote a "humble petition" to the excise service,
requesting reinstatement. The petition was granted, and he

took up a new post in the town of Lewes, south of London. On April 8, 1774, after six stormy years, he was definitively fired from the excise service for failure to follow regulations.

The emotions that shook him now were suffused with paranoia. Picking his way through a host of enemies, he finally decided that the authority who was responsible for all his misfortunes with the government was no one else than George III. "A king who could dismiss a loyal and able servant must certainly be either stupid or wicked or both."

In the process of venting his spleen against a father figure who had dismissed him rather than forgiven him, as Joseph Pain had always done, he finally found his profession. Less than two years after losing his job, he became internationally famous by dint of telling the American colonists, in unforgettably scorching language, how completely he "rejected the hardened, sullen-tempered Pharaoh of England," how thoroughly he disdained "the wretch, that with pretended title of *Father of his People* can unfeelingly hear of their slaughter, and composedly sleep with their blood upon his soul."[10]

CHARLES COTESWORTH PINCKNEY was born in 1745, the first of three children of Charles Pinckney, a plantation owner and lawyer in South Carolina, and of his remarkable second wife, Eliza. In her young womanhood, Eliza had managed her father's plantation during his long absences in the West Indies. She also played a leading role in introducing indigo into the agriculture of South Carolina. As prospective parents, Charles and Eliza Pinckney studied all the modern methods of child rearing. Finally they concluded that the best way to bring up Charles Cotesworth was to induce him to "play himself into learning." To this end, Charles Pinckney designed and built a set of toys which, he hoped, would help his son to recognize the letters of the alphabet. The toys proved to be a great success. The boy recognized all twenty-six letters before he could properly pronounce them, and began to spell words before he was two years old.

Charles Cotesworth's younger brother and sister were given similar opportunities to develop rapidly during their first years of life. But as the children moved out of infancy, their father devoted himself more exclusively to his two sons. In 1753 he moved his family to England, so that the two boys could be educated there. Living in England proved so congenial to the family that Charles and Eliza decided to settle there permanently. Accordingly, they went back to Charleston in order to dispose of Charles' investments, leaving the boys behind to continue their studies. Shortly after arriving in Charleston, Charles was stricken with a fatal illness. Instead of returning to England, the widowed Eliza remained in South Carolina to oversee the family's finances.

As Marvin R. Zahniser observes in his biography of Charles Cotesworth, Eliza never allowed the image of their father to grow dim in the minds of his sons. In a typical letter, she reminded them that "He has set you a great and good example, may the Lord enable you both to follow it. . . ." Because he was the elder son, Charles Cotesworth was called upon with particular vehemence to prove himself worthy of his heritage. "You must know," Eliza wrote to him, "the welfair of a whole family depends in great measure on the progress you make. . . ." Yet at the same time that she sent him hortatory letters, she recognized that as the male heir he could do as he pleased. In choosing to study at Christ Church, Oxford, at the Middle Temple in London, and at the Royal Military College in Caen, France, Charles Cotesworth carried out his father's and mother's plans for him. But the choices were his to make. At every point in his young manhood, a sense of freedom intermingled with a sense of obligation.

Returning to South Carolina in 1769, he became, in the words of another Charleston patriot, "an early, decided and devoted prompter of the revolution." As for his motives, his biographer makes clear that he did not turn against the British because Crown policies had damaged his financial interests.

On the contrary, he had little to gain by being anti-British, and a great deal to lose if he were to side with a revolutionary movement that went down to defeat. As Pinckney himself said, he joined the Revolution on principle. While it was his nature to be loyal, his dutifulness could not be compelled.[11]

DAVID RITTENHOUSE was born and grew up on a hundred-acre farm three miles above the Schuylkill River and twenty miles from Philadelphia. His father, Matthias, had a German Mennonite background; his mother came from a Welsh Quaker family. Ten children issued from their marriage, of whom David was the second child and first son.

Mrs. Rittenhouse was a deeply religious, poorly educated woman, narrow in her interests and rigid in her habits. A casual observer might have concluded that her husband was an equally limited person. In appearance he seemed to be a typical Pennsylvania Dutch farmer, self-sustaining, respectable, hard-working, and set in his ways. Brooke Hindle, the biographer of David Rittenhouse, makes the point, though, that in his early life Matthias had demonstrated much more adaptability and fortitude than a casual observer was likely to see. He had not been raised to be a farmer, but had been associated from childhood with his father and brothers in the operation of a family-owned paper mill near the Wissahickon River. When his older brother inherited both the mill and the solid stone house built by their grandfather, Matthias indignantly withdrew from the papermaking business and sought a world elsewhere. In his new life as a farmer he did extraordinarily well, despite his lack of experience.

Much of young David's early education was given to him by his father. Through this association the boy acquired aspirations and attitudes that stayed with him for the rest of his life. But when David began to show an inordinate interest in a carpenter's box of tools and some elementary mathematics books that had been left with him by one of his uncles, Matthias' first reaction was to oppose his son. He thought of his eldest son as his successor; therefore he could not be permitted to while away his days building wooden models of water mills and tinkering with clocks. Perhaps it was during this frustrating time that David learned to keep his surging emotions under an iron control, and began to suffer from the pain of a chronic ulcer. Eventually, the flexibility which Matthias had demonstrated in his own change of careers came to the rescue of his son's unorthodox ambitions. Matthias not only permitted David to give up farming, but bought him the tools he would need to become a professional clockmaker. In addition, he allowed his son to build a workshop on the edge of the farm, alongside the road to town. From the age of eighteen until the outbreak of the Revolution, the future orrery builder and astronomer made clocks for a living.

In his spare time he was an active patriot, for Rittenhouse's commitment to the cause of American rights was "complete and irrevocable," in Brooke Hindle's words. The clockmaker's disgust with the British reached new heights at the time of the Boston Tea Party, and thereafter he was directly caught up in the struggle for freedom.[12]

ANTHONY WAYNE was the grandson of Captain Anthony Wayne, who fought with Marlborough in the Continental wars and was a leader of King William's dragoons at the Battle of the Boyne. His career as a soldier ended, Captain Wayne emigrated to America and settled on a farm of 380 acres in fertile Chester County, Pennsylvania. The nearby settlement of Waynesborough was named for the old hero.

One of Captain Wayne's sons, a tough, plain-spoken boy named Isaac, grew up to become the leader of the local militia and an assemblyman from Chester County, as well as a prosperous farmer. His Quaker wife gave birth to a son in 1745, and Isaac named the infant after his now-dead grandfather.

In his childhood, young Anthony Wayne was told that he had the hot temper of the man he was named for, and the same pugnaciously jutting jaw. Nevertheless, Isaac did not want his son to follow in his grandfather's footsteps. He aimed Anthony toward a legal rather than a military career.

The boy, however, had no interest in books. The school he attended was run by his Uncle Gilbert, who repeatedly informed the boy's father that his son was not doing well. "Your affection blinds you, Brother Isaac," Gilbert wrote him on one occasion. "You mistake your son's capacity. I cannot tell what occupation suits him best, but I am certain that he will never make a scholar. . . . Unless Anthony pays more attention to his books, I shall be under the painful necessity of dismissing him from school." Stung by his brother's frankness, Isaac insisted that Anthony be permitted to remain. But the situation did not improve. Except for Caesar's account of his military campaigns, Latin bored the boy. What he mainly liked to do at school was to play soldiers in the yard with the other boys. In these war games, Anthony Wayne was always the leader.

Finally his father heeded Gilbert's advice and removed him from the school. Yet Isaac still believed that his son could become an academic success if he wanted to. He therefore arranged to send him to the Philadelphia Academy. Perhaps the change of scene would inspire him to improve his study habits. He also wrote his son a stern letter, outlining the dire consequences of another failure. "It is, my son, the last chance I shall give you. If you do not persevere, I shall take you out of school and send you to do the harshest labor on the farm." But as Wayne's biographer, Harry Emerson Wildes, points out, Anthony's father was "concealing indulgence under a mask of harshness." The truth of the matter was that Isaac had no intention of imposing his own dream of a good life upon his son, if his son was clearly uninterested in a legal career.

The historic Blue Ball Tavern on the Lancaster Road provided the occasion for a negotiated settlement between Isaac and Anthony. The tavern had long served as a meeting place for military officers, and young Anthony was irresistibly drawn to it. Here he talked to captains and lieutenants who were on their way to give battle to the French at Fort Duquesne. He learned from these men that mathematics, engineering, and surveying were essential elements of military knowledge. Returning home, Anthony told his father that he would work hard at the Philadelphia Academy, provided that he could concentrate less on Latin and more on science. His father agreed to this proposition, and further promised that he would purchase a commission for Anthony in one of the better Guards regiments. Out of mutual respect, father and son sought for and reached a reconciliation of their differences.[13]

The men who broke with Britain in 1776 had been prepared by their upbringings to make a successful separation from their parents and to face with equanimity the prospect of living independently. The psychologically painful enterprise of overthrowing the father figure of George III and of breaking the historic connection between the colonies and the imperial parens patriae was led by colonists who had not been tyrannized over by their own fathers, and who in fact were accustomed to thinking of paternal authority as the guarantor of filial freedom and self-realization. Both of the foregoing sentences apply to the patriots we have just been considering.

So satisfying, indeed, was their experience with their fathers that it has caused me to wonder whether father-son relations in the Revolutionary generation did not mark a special moment in the history of the American family; certainly in no other period of our past can we find the top leaders of American society speaking as gratefully as these patriots did about the fathering they had received.

The reasons for their gratitude are not hard to understand. To begin with, their fathers were a daily presence in their lives, because the work of the family breadwinner was performed at home or close by. In the absence of schools and tutors, their fathers also offered them formal instruction, which lent further meaning to the relationship between them. These arrangements, of course, were historically familiar ones in the colonial American household. However, the disciplinary methods employed by the fathers of the men under discussion here exemplify Oscar and Mary Handlin's contention, in their fascinating study of youth and the family in American history, that the power of the head of the household in eighteenth-century America had become a qualified authority. Taking their stand somewhere between the rigid authoritarianism of the seventeenth century and the lack of structure and of limit setting characteristic of a later America, these fathers saddled their sons with serious responsibilities at a very young age, at the same time that they loosened the reins and let them run free. If the sons sometimes found themselves at loggerheads with their fathers, the conflicts were generally resolved by some sort of mutually satisfactory compromise. Even those conflicts which were settled by paternal fiat did not result in filial resentment—or if they did, then the resentment was repressed, emerging later as an aggressiveness toward other people. For the biographical record we have been looking at is strikingly devoid of evidence of enduring ill will between fathers and sons. The generations understood one another, even when their values and points of view diverged, and in their intense commitment to personal advancement and achievement they found a common purpose. Time and again, during the recent bicentennial celebration of American independence, editorial writers and other observers of the American scene kept coming back to the mystery of how a population of just over 2 million white people managed to produce such outstanding leadership in such impressive depth. Obviously no single factor can account for this phenomenon, but I would suggest that the quality of the relationship between the patriot leaders and their fathers had something to do with it. In saying this I certainly do not mean to imply, as

Parson Weems did in his egregious biography of George Washington, that the fathers of the Revolutionary leaders shaped their sons into flawless human beings. On the contrary, a good many of the leaders were unpleasantly abrasive men who became even more unpleasant when they were crossed. John Adams always wanted to be first, no matter what the competition was; John Hancock was as willful as he was empty-headed; Patrick Henry, as Jefferson avowed, was "avaritious & rotten hearted."[14] In revolutions, after all, it is not the meek who inherit the earth. As Chairman Mao used to say, a social uprising is not a dinner party.

Projecting backward from twentieth-century experience, we would expect to discover that the strong sense of entitlement which marked so many of the personalities we have just been considering was traceable to strong mothering. However, the historical evidence—such as it is—does not confirm this expectation. A few mothers, most notably Eliza Pinckney, played demonstrably important roles in their sons' development, but they did so in the face of circumstances which seem to have defeated many other women. For while the lot of the American mother in the eighteenth century was better than it had been a century earlier, she still did not share her husband's economic and political rights. If she was a partner in a co-operative parental effort, she clearly was the subordinate partner, whose decisions were subject to review. She was also expected to bear half a dozen, a dozen, or even a dozen and a half children. Not surprisingly, many men buried two, three, or four wives in the course of their marital careers. The eighteenth-century mother was also discriminated against as far as her education was concerned, and had been exposed in early life to a much more constricted personal experience than her husband. Consequently she was apt to be less sophisticated and more conservative than her spouse; if paternal authority had not ruled the roost, she would have imposed a greater restraint on the freedom of her male children. The result of all this, in some of the families of the Revolutionary generation at any rate, was a considerable tension between mothers and sons, which caused the latter to view the former as sharp-tongued termagants to be avoided whenever possible, or as hopeless ignoramuses who could not talk intelligently about anything important. The very fact that we have no evidence at all about the mothering of most patriots may also tell us something about the quality of mother-son relations in the Revolutionary generation. Or does the lack of evidence simply mean that mothers constituted the background against which all the events in the early lives of their children occurred, and that the reason why historians cannot see them is that they were everywhere?

In any event, when we look at Thomas Jefferson and George Washington, as I would now like to do, we see that even after the untimely death of their fathers, whom they admired enormously, they did not draw any closer to their mothers. Instead, they turned to other men, for what they were primarily interested in was a perpetuation of the sort of father-son relationship that had meant so much to them in childhood.

THOMAS JEFFERSON was the son of Peter Jefferson, a man of giant proportions and fabulous strength who was in his vigorous middle thirties when his third child and first son was born in 1743. Although he performed prodigious deeds as a surveyor of unexplored territory, the elder Jefferson was at no time a typical frontiersman, as Dumas Malone has made clear. He owned slaves. He owned impressive pieces of property, in the populous district below the James River as well as in the more sparsely settled Piedmont. His closest friends were influential figures in the power structure of the Old Dominion. His wife was a Randolph.

As a Virginia aristocrat, Thomas Jefferson was not indifferent to his distinguished lineage. Nevertheless he was prouder of his father than of any other ancestor, for reasons having nothing to do with Peter Jefferson's affiliation with the Old Dominion elite. He admired him rather for his awesome physical strength which enabled him to "head up" two hogsheads of tobacco at the same time, for his keen if uneducated intelligence, for his bold decision to build a home in the Southwest Mountains, and for his exploits as a surveyor of boundaries in the primeval wilderness. Not easily given to words, Peter Jefferson let his actions speak for him, and his literarily gifted son regarded him as a storybook hero. "In his early history," says Dumas Malone, Thomas Jefferson "would have made Peter Jefferson the dominant character."

Despite or perhaps because of his own lack of learning, Peter Jefferson tried to make sure that Thomas received the best education that Virginia could offer. In 1752, when he was nine, the boy was placed in a boarding school in Northam. Although he prospered at the school, Thomas missed his home. Whether he specifically missed his mother is not clear. Indeed, it is not clear how actively involved Jane Randolph Jefferson was at any point in the upbringing of her first son. She bore ten children altogether, of whom eight survived, and her energies were further drained by the changes of domicile which her restless husband insisted on. In later life the only comment that Thomas Jefferson is known to have made about his mother's influence on him was uncomplimentary. The fact that he never at any point sought the advice of women about problems that seriously concerned him was probably another indication of his fundamental lack of respect for his mother's opinions. He was very much his father's boy.

Thus when Peter Jefferson suddenly died in August 1757, it was a traumatic event for his fourteen-year-old son. Although in many ways he was quite grown up, Thomas still felt a need for paternal guidance, but there was no relative or family friend or teacher whom he trusted in that special sense. In later life he would recall the emotionally devastating summer of his father's death and assert that from that point onward the "whole care and direction of his life were thrown on himself."

For two and a half years, the boy quietly carried the burden of his loneliness. Finally, in the spring of 1760, shortly after enrolling at the College of William and Mary, he encountered a professor of natural philosophy, named William Small, who probably fixed the destinies of his life, as Jefferson afterward averred. The only layman on the faculty, Small was a spokesman for Enlightenment ideas. To the young undergraduate, Small's intellectual skepticism and spiritual receptivity were a revelation. But as Dumas Malone has shown, what Jefferson mainly learned from Small was not obedience to the authority of a learned professor, but delight in the free play of his own mind. On a personal level, Small made an equally important impact on Jefferson. An unmarried and lonely man, Small was as grateful for Jefferson's companionship as Jefferson was for his. In the course of their many informal meetings, Jefferson observed that Small pursued an "even and dignified" line of conduct in a disorderly world. On the one hand, he did not seek to recover his lost youth by involving himself in the student brawls that periodically rocked the college. But on the other hand he was the only member of the faculty who, in Dumas Malone's words, "denied the arbitrary power of a master to inflict punishment on an offending scholar." Like the fathers of John Adams, Anthony Wayne, and other future leaders of the American Revolution, Professor Small believed that young personalities required a mixture of freedom and authority. It is no wonder that Jefferson regarded Small as "like a father" to him.[15]

GEORGE WASHINGTON also looked up to a father possessed of remarkable physical strength. In James Thomas Flexner's words, Augustine Washington was "a blond giant, fabulously strong, but miraculously gentle." Although he probably served as young George's teacher for a time, Augustine was surely a more effective parent when he and his son pushed aside their books and ventured out of doors. George's daringly graceful horsemanship, his prowess as a player of rough sports, and his amazing feats of strength were the activities that put him in touch with his father. For Augustine was much less sure of himself as a thinker than as a doer. In his numerous land-speculation deals, for example, he proved to be a rather nervous businessman, given to indecisiveness and delay, and susceptible to law suits.

Augustine married twice. By his first wife he had three children. After her death he married Mary Ball and sired several more, of whom George was the oldest. Mary Ball's father had died when she was three and her mother when she was twelve. Without parents to guide her or education to enlighten her, she developed into an extremely self-centered woman. In later years Mary Washington tended to alarm the people who came into her majestic presence, because they sensed, correctly, that she was easily displeased. Such was his mother's egotism that "whatever George attempted that was not in her immediate service," Flexner says, "she attempted to stop." Thus she was rather nettled by her son's rise to fame. Although she was in excellent health, she never left home to witness any of the ceremonies that honored him. Whenever she was told how much the American people admired and appreciated George's achievements, she was apt to run him down—and this was not modesty. During the Revolution she let it be known that a certain famous general was so forgetful of his filial duties that his widowed mother was in danger of starving to death. In all likelihood, the ensuing publicity pleased her as much as it infuriated and embarrassed the general.

Growing up in a farmhouse on the Rappahannock, which contained six rooms, numerous children, and his mother, young George found relief from intramural tensions in extended visits to relatives in Westmoreland County, and to his half-brother Lawrence's home at Mount Vernon. The harassed youth may even have welcomed his father's idea of sending him to school in England, although he was certainly no scholar. But when Augustine died in 1743, the idea of England died with him. At age eleven, George Washington was driven back on his own ability to defend his individuality. In this effort he was aided and abetted by Lawrence. Almost a generation older than George, Lawrence was more than just his half-brother's "best friend," as George described him. Lawrence had been educated in England and had seen action as a captain in the British regular army in Spain. Good-humored and charming, this tall, sallow-complexioned man was also serious and responsible. He supplemented the lessons George received from a private tutor and at a nearby school, and probably talked to the boy about the problems he had encountered in his various capacities as the president of the land-speculating Ohio Company, the adjutant general of Virginia, and the local representative to the legislature in Williamsburg. In these and other ways he played a paternal role in the life of a fatherless adolescent. "Effective yet sweet and gentle," Flexner says, "he inspired in his younger brother a passionate devotion." When the consumption from which Lawrence chronically suffered became acute, George accompanied him to a warm springs, and later went with him to Barbados, in the hope that the Caribbean climate would alleviate the illness. Lawrence's death in 1752 seems to have upset George even more than the death of his father had.

Yet it did not take Lawrence's passing to shock George Washington into maturity, for the twenty-year-old youth had long since left his boyhood behind him. Toward the end of his formal schooling, five or six years earlier, he had become fascinated by the problems of surveying. The life of a surveyor appealed to his logical mind as well as to his adventuresome imagination, and as Flexner points out, it also offered him an excuse for leaving home. When the wealthy Fairfax family, whom he had met through Lawrence, hired a surveyor to lay out lots in the Shenandoah Valley, George Washington, age sixteen, was invited to join the expedition—

and Lawrence gave him permission to go. Paddling a canoe forty miles in a day, against the current and under a pelting rain, pushed the young Washington to the limit of his endurance, but left him with an appetite for even more arduous tests. In the spring of 1750 he entered the wild, mountainous country of western Virginia and surveyed forty-seven tracts, for which he was paid a fee of almost £140. With the money he bought a likely piece of land he had come across near Bullskin Creek, a tributary of the Shenandoah. At nineteen he was not only a blazer of wilderness trails, but a land speculator, like Augustine and Lawrence.

George also aspired to fill Lawrence's shoes as adjutant general of Virginia, and after much politicking was appointed adjutant of the Northern Neck. In 1753, the twenty-one-year-old Washington was commanded by Lieutenant Governor Dinwiddie to undertake an assignment of global significance. He was to push into the wilderness and establish contact with friendly Indians, whom he would then persuade to tell him where the French were. Once he had received this information, he was to proceed to the main French base, determine the number of the enemy's troops and the extent of their line of fortifications, and present a letter from Dinwiddie to their commanding officer, demanding the withdrawal of all French forces from territories claimed by the British Crown. "It was deemed by some," Washington laconically commented many years later, "an extraordinary circumstance that so young and inexperienced a person should have been employed on a negotiation with which subjects of the greatest importance were involved." Five years after his surrogate father had given him permission to go surveying in the wilderness, George Washington had emerged on the stage of world events, in the forefront of an extraordinary generation of Americans.[16]

When Charles Cotesworth Pinckney's father died, he continued to live in his son's mind, through the eloquent efforts of Charles Cotesworth's sympathetic mother, Eliza. Thomas Jefferson and George Washington, however, were alienated from their mothers. When their fathers died, they both set out on their own to find new sources of paternal inspiration—and they succeeded. Thus their early lives constitute a variation on, but not a departure from, the basic pattern I have discerned in the early lives of other patriots. Like their most famous Revolutionary comrades, Jefferson and Washington drew strength when they needed it from strong but not overbearing father figures.

If my evidence ended here, then I could say as I did at the close of the chapter on loyalist backgrounds that, while my sample is small, it contains no exceptions. However, the fact is that among the biographies which contain meaningful descriptions of the early lives of patriot Americans, I did find three cases that do not fit my argument. As we now shall see, the fathers of William Livingston and James Otis exercised a stifling control over their sons, while Alexander Hamilton's father abandoned his paternal responsibilities altogether. In terms of the contrasting patterns I have been developing, these three men may be said to have had "loyalist" rather than "patriot" childhoods.

ALEXANDER HAMILTON had good cause to feel anxious and angry about his father. Not only did James Hamilton neglect to marry Rachael Lavien, the mother of his two sons, but after moving his family to the island of St. Croix in 1765, he returned alone to the island of St. Kitts and in all probability never saw either mistress or children again. Alexander was barely ten years old at the time. The kind of strong fathering which had a major influence on the personalities of other patriots was not a factor in Hamilton's early life.

James Hamilton's irresponsibility, however, was coupled with an undeniable charm. Alexander in particular felt an attachment to him, which was not broken by James's departure. Even though there were probably no reunions between them, Alexander continued for the rest of his boyhood to write letters to his father, which were full of affectionate sympathy for his growing financial difficulties. For the elder Hamilton's various efforts to make money were unprofitable and ultimately drove him into bankruptcy. After moving to the mainland in 1772, Alexander often lost touch with his father for long periods, but showed concern for him and sent him money whenever he could. Between 1796 and 1799, he remitted several thousand dollars to James. That the son bore no bitterness toward the father was testimony to the fact that James's desertion of his family in 1765 had not destroyed the people he left behind.

Rachael Lavien was a strong and resourceful woman. She had well-to-do relatives to whom she could have turned in her plight, but she scorned the thought of being a burden to them. Instead, she opened a small store in Christiansted, St. Croix, and put her sons to work as well. In all likelihood, the ten-year-old Alexander helped his mother to wait on customers and balance accounts. By giving the boy this sort of responsibility, Rachael encouraged him to grow up fast. The policy was even wiser than she knew, for in 1768 Rachael unexpectedly died. At age thirteen the bereft Alexander "looked at his world with the candid eyes of a man," as one of his biographers has written.

It was probably in the months following his mother's death that Alexander was hired as a clerk by Beckman & Cruger, a leading export-import firm in Christiansted. The firm provided him with a livelihood, and much more. For Nicholas Cruger in effect became his father. The remarkably rewarding tension between paternal discipline and filial autonomy that characterized the father-son relationships of other boys who became leaders of the American Revolution now began to apply, somewhat belatedly, to Alexander Hamilton. As far as his education was concerned, he had received a smattering of learning from his mother, but it is believed that he did not receive any formal instruction until he moved to the mainland. Yet Cruger's counting house was in a very real sense a school, in which Nicholas Cruger was the teacher. Legally speaking, Alexander was just an apprentice, but as soon as he learned how the sugar-export business worked, Cruger gave him sole authority for the purchase and sale of several cargoes. And when Cruger went to the mainland on an extended business trip in 1771, he left Alexander behind to cope with ship captains, planters, merchants, lawyers, and an assorted array of managerial headaches, even though the boy was not yet seventeen. Moreover, his surrogate father gave Alexander his first lessons in politics. A thoroughgoing Whig with close family and business connections in New York City, Cruger was an ardent supporter of the American colonists' protests against imperial interference. In 1779, one of his cargoes was confiscated and condemned by the British, and he himself imprisoned. Four years later, he served as chairman of the committee that escorted General Washington on his triumphal entrance into New York.

It was probably during long conversations after business hours in the late 1760s and early 1770s that Cruger imparted his political ideas to a most attentive listener. After it became apparent to the older man that his young associate had a mind that could benefit from a more philosophical training than he could give him, he brought together a group of well-to-do men in Christiansted to underwrite Hamilton's education on the mainland. Cruger himself, though, along with his business partner Cornelius Kortright, was the youth's chief benefactor, as of course he had been for the preceding four years.

In America, the brilliant young man from the Caribbean aroused the fatherly interest of William Livingston and Elias Boudinot. But while their interest was flattering and useful, he did not really need to be looked after. The process of preparing Alexander Hamilton to take care of himself had long since been completed. "His responsibilities as Cruger's deputy," writes Broadus Mitchell, "had thrown him in touch with the principal figures of the island, whether in private or in public life. He had known and dealt with men in authority, at least such as was there wielded. His attitude was deferential but not diffident. He arrived in America with the aura of personages worn off."

Like all the Revolutionary leaders, Hamilton came to manhood very quickly. Nevertheless his precocity was remarkable. In 1776 he was twenty-one years old and the captain of an artillery company. At twenty-two he joined George Washington's general staff.[17]

WILLIAM LIVINGSTON was born in 1723, the eighth child of the rich New York merchant and landowner Philip Livingston. Much of William's childhood was spent in the care of his maternal grandmother, Sarah Van Brugh. There was a family theory that his irascibility of temper in later life resulted from the "excessive fondness and indiscriminating indulgence" of Grandmother Van Brugh's supervision of him. His own memories of her were quite different, however. Although he remembered his grandmother affectionately, he stressed the industry, efficiency, and morality of her household. It was not indulgence he recalled, but "wholesome precepts."

In any event, his father also took an active interest in William's upbringing. "I do not bring any of my Sons up for Idleness," Philip Livingston announced, "but to mind some employment or other." Otherwise, he said, "Youth are deluded and brought over to bad company [and] begett ill vices from w[hich] I pray God to preserve them." Once the elder Livingston had decided that William should enter the family business in Albany, William did so forthwith. Yet when William showed neither a taste nor an aptitude for the mysteries of mercantilism, his father humored his request that he not be required to make a career as a businessman. The emboldened youth then suggested that he would like to follow up the literary interests he had developed as a Yale undergraduate by studying painting. This time his father turned him down flat. While there was a certain freedom of choice in the Livingston household, it had definite limits. Painting was impractical, said the elder Livingston, and besides, he needed a lawyer he could trust. Reluctantly, William agreed to fill his father's need, but never ceased to wish that he had more time for poetry and art. Possibly it was artistic frustration that precipitated his famous irascibility.

In William Livingston's relations with his father, the balance between freedom and authority tipped more often toward authority than it did in the experience of his two patriot brothers, Philip and Peter. William's mixed success in doing what he wanted with his life rather than what his father desired for him was eventually reflected in the ambivalence of his politics. He wanted America to be free of tyranny—but the prospect of independence made him nervous. Unaware of his inner turmoil, his Whig friends were surprised when he opposed the Declaration of Independence. After the delegates in Philadelphia made their fateful decision, however, he accepted it. Toward the end of the summer of 1776, William Livingston assumed the governorship of Revolutionary New Jersey.[18]

JAMES OTIS was raised by a domineering father who had no wish to stop running his son's life even after he was grown up. Where other patriots could conceivably have seen a contrast between their own fathers' restrained use of power and the efforts of the imperial parent in London to impose new and humiliating regulations upon the American colonies, Otis most definitely did not. Far from clarifying and intensifying his revolutionary resentments, Otis' childish memories left him stricken with the awareness that the tyrannies of George III and James Otis, Sr., were very much alike. Thus the more he thought about overthrowing British rule, the more it loomed in his mind as a crime of parricide. Throughout the 1760s, Otis' love-hate relationship with his father repeatedly confused and disrupted his attempts to formulate a philosophically coherent criticism of Britain's interference in colonial affairs. In 1771, a tormented, guilt-ridden man suffered a shattering mental breakdown. He played no part in the American Revolution because he was non compos mentis.

James Otis, Sr., married Mary Allyne in 1724. In the course of the next twenty years, Otis made his wife pregnant thirteen times. James, Jr., their first child, was born in 1725. Because of his position as the eldest child and namesake son, young James was exposed even more brutally than his younger brothers were to the fanatical determination of their father to perpetuate a dynasty.

As John J. Waters, Jr., has observed in his brilliant study *The Otis Family in Provincial and Revolutionary Massachusetts*, a way of life, a set of values, a pattern of interests connected father to son in this family of Barnstable, Massachusetts, merchants across four generations. Fathers worked hard and accumulated wealth in the expectation that their sons would do the same for their sons. Just as James Otis, Sr., had inherited his father's glittering sword and silver-topped cane, so he intended to bequeath these symbols of patriarchal authority to James, Jr. But that event lay far off in the future. The elder Otis intended to live a long life, and in the meantime his namesake and his younger sons Joseph and Samuel would work for the mercantile and political glory of the Otises under their father's ceaseless supervision. Thus he controlled the whole question of his sons' education. If James, Jr., was permitted to go to Harvard, it was because the elder Otis considered a college education a good investment for the family to make, especially since he carefully deducted all of young James's Harvard expenses from his family inheritance.

In 1748, having finished college and read law, young James established a legal practice in Plymouth, Massachusetts. This did not mean, however, that he had at last freed himself from his father's surveillance, for the elder Otis was himself a lawyer, and Plymouth was not so far from Barnstable that he could not maintain his usual level of interference in whatever his son was doing. In the words of John J. Waters, Jr., his father "sent James the proper executions, cautioned on charging fees, asked him to represent him in small matters, and did everything but give James the independence that he wanted."

Hot-tempered, suspicious, manipulative, and overbearing, the elder Otis came to be regarded by all his sons as a menace to their integrity. At the same time, they recognized that their own success in life owed a good deal to the advantages he had put in their way, as well as to the driving ambition he had instilled in them. They also could not help partaking in their father's pride in being an Otis, even though they realized that their individuality was threatened by the mystique of the family. All the Otis brothers were consequently caught in a crossfire of emotions. One of the evidences of their unsettled state of mind was the frequency with which they quarreled with one another. Doubtless their competitive natures made for friction between them, but as Waters says, "the mutual bickerings, fears and hostilities of these brothers" basically testified to "their insecurity before the dominating personality of their father."

Ambivalent feelings about the senior Otis had a more dire effect on James, Jr., than on his brothers. The depressing sense that he was being victimized by powerful forces came to dominate his adult imagination, but even during childhood and adolescence his disposition was so moody and his mind so excitable that friends wondered how stable he was. A particularly disturbing episode from his Harvard days has been recounted by Otis' nineteenth-century biographer William Tudor. Home from college, Otis was persuaded by a group of friends to play a country dance on his violin. While the friends were cavorting to the music, "Otis suddenly stopped and holding up his fiddle and bow exclaimed 'So Orpheus fiddled, and so danced the brutes!' and then tossing aside the instrument, rushed into the garden, followed by the disappointed revellers."

The wild and whirling passion of his oratory, as well as his impressive legal learning, quickly brought young Otis to the forefront of the political struggle against imperial intrusions into American life, a struggle in which the senior Otis was also engaged. Yet the young Otis' thrilling speeches were full of contradictions. On the one hand he believed in American rights, but on the other hand was horrified by the thought of independence. Separation from the parent state, he fervently declared, "every good and honest man would wish delayed for ages, if possible, prevented for ever." And while he did not hesitate to hurl historically untenable accusations of constitutional illegality against Parliament, he was conspicuously silent about the faults of the king, the symbolic father.

Otis' sister Mercy was conscious of what a tortured and self-doubting man her brilliant brother was, and cast him as the Brutus character in a patriotic play she wrote. If, however, she had been a more sensitive and insightful writer, her portrayal would have indicated that James' contradictory political views were entangled in unresolved personal problems. It would remain for John J. Waters, Jr., to suggest that the image of George III had fused in Otis' feverish mind with the image of James Otis, Sr. "After all, had not the elder Otis been both king and tyrant, father and antagonist to his own sons?"

As events pushed him toward anti-British positions, which increased his sense of danger and his feelings of guilt, Otis began to behave more and more abnormally. One night in a tavern an officer of the king accused him of being an enemy to the "rights of the crown and disaffected to his Majesty." Otis was so enraged or so frightened by this coarse formulation of his complicated feelings that he fought with the officer and suffered a head injury that may have done further damage to his mind. In a move that was shocking in a different way, he gave up his celebrated law practice. He also confessed to a doctor, as the political tension continued to heighten, that all of his political recommendations had been wrong, that America faced certain ruin, that he himself was on the edge of death, and that he was afraid to die. *"Cursed be the day I was born,"* his confession concluded. He now began to drink heavily. His conversation became defiled by "Trash, Obsceneness, Profaneness and Distraction." He broke the windows of a building, and broke the Sabbath by firing off guns.

His father's reaction to his son's behavior was to rebuke him for it, and to place the blame for his mental illness on young James's failure to be sufficiently religious. The elder Otis also said that he had done everything in the world for his son, and was now being rewarded by conduct calculated to add gray hairs to his head and drive him to his grave.

In 1771, the family decided that young James had to be confined. When the Revolution came, the invalid began to pray that God the Father would strike him dead by a bolt of lightning. In 1783, he died the way he had wished.[19]

The argument could be made, I suppose, that Alexander Hamilton's childhood qualifies for inclusion in the pattern of "patriot" childhoods, because of his strong if belated relationship with Nicholas Cruger. The fact that the early lives of William Livingston and James Otis do not fit the pattern might be explained away on the grounds that Livingston's opposition to the Declaration of Independence and Otis' psychological inability to face up to the revolutionary events of the 1770s also deviated from the patriotic norm. I am not, however, inclined to quibble. My research uncovered three exceptional cases. Whatever they may show, they do not constitute a large-enough number to damage the significance of the other cases we have been examining, or to vitiate the force of the questions that they raise. Were the men who made the American Revolution—I guess I should say, were *most* of the men who made the American Revolution—bound together as a group by the kind of relationship they had had in childhood with their fathers? Did memories of their fathers' restrained use of power affect their adult perception of the colonial-imperial relationship? Was their willingness, in the end, to take the awesome risk of revolting against the armed might of Great Britain grounded in a childish self-confidence? The evidence I have assembled here is not massive enough to permit me to answer these questions. Nevertheless, the haunting possibility exists that the answer in every case is: yes.

Notes

1. Page Smith, *John Adams* (Garden City, N. Y., 1962), I, pp. 3-57. See also John Adams, *Diary and Autobiography,* ed. Lyman Butterfield, 4 vols. (Cambridge, Mass., 1961).

2. John C. Miller, *Sam Adams. Pioneer in Propaganda* (Boston, 1936), pp. 4-22.

3. Joseph Gurn, *Charles Carroll of Carrollton. 1737-1832* (New York, 1932), pp. 3-80.

4. Carl Van Doren, *Benjamin Franklin* (New York, 1961), pp. 7-33. [Originally published 1938.] See also Benjamin Franklin, *Autobiography* (Boston, 1966), pp. 1-18.

5. Theodore Thayer, *Nathanael Greene. Strategist of the American Revolution* (New York, 1960), pp. 15-22.

6. Herbert S. Allan, *John Hancock. Patriot in Purple* (New York, 1948), pp. 26-81.

7. Richard R. Beeman, *Patrick Henry. A Biography* (New York, 1974), pp. 2-36.

8. Irving Brant, *James Madison. The Virginia Revolutionist* (Indianapolis, 1941), pp. 26-196.

9. Albert J. Beveridge, *The Life of John Marshall* (Boston, 1916), I, pp. 7-68.

10. David Freeman Hawke, *Paine* (New York, 1974), pp. 7-19.

11. Marvin R. Zahniser, *Charles Cotesworth Pinckney. Founding Father* (Chapel Hill, 1967), pp. 6-45.

12. Brooke Hindle, *David Rittenhouse* (Princeton, 1964), pp. 11-123.

13. Harry Emerson Wildes, *Anthony Wayne. Trouble Shooter of the American Revolution* (Westport, Conn., 1970), pp. 3-14. [Originally published 1941.]

14. Beeman, p. xii.

15. Dumas Malone, *Jefferson the Virginian* (Boston, 1948), pp. 4-42, 52-55.

16. James Thomas Flexner, *George Washington. The Forge of Experience (1732-1775)* (Boston, 1965), pp. 5-56.

17. Broadus Mitchell, *Alexander Hamilton. Youth to Maturity 1755-1788* (New York, 1962), pp. 8-72. [Originally published 1957.]

18. Milton Martin Klein, "The American Whig: William Livingston of New York" (Ph.D. diss. Columbia University, 1954), pp. 37-39, 71, 72, 707-08.

19. John J. Waters, Jr., *The Otis Family in Provincial and Revolutionary Massachusetts* (Chapel Hill, 1968), pp. 63-198. William Tudor, *The Life of James Otis* (Boston, 1823), pp. 9, 364-65.

CHAPTER THREE

A Divided People

To the victors belong the spoils of historical interpretation. In the wake of the Revolution, the historians of a triumphant republic enlarged upon the idea of wartime propagandists that the American colonists had been united in their struggle against British oppression. At no point in their mythmaking works did Mercy Otis Warren, Parson Weems, or David Ramsay acknowledge the true extent of disunity in Revolutionary America. Nor did they attempt to define what the patriots had in common as opposed to what the loyalists had in common, or to explain how the shared characteristics of each group led to its fateful choice of allegiance in 1776. The only message that the post-Revolutionary writers wished to convey to posterity was that the war against the British had been spontaneously and enthusiastically supported by a nation of heroes. If Weems and company mentioned the loyalists, it was only in order to crush the infamy of Machiavellian plotters and shameless toadies.

Throughout the nineteenth century, historians of the Revolution continued to give evasive answers to the fundamentally important question of why the colonists had been divided. In his massive and enormously influential *History of the United States,* George Bancroft saw the rebellion against George III as part of a vast pageant of freedom. Bancroft believed that Americans had an inborn—i.e., God-given—love of liberty, and that their history proved it. No sooner was Jamestown settled in 1607 than the colonists began to resist arbitrary British interference in their affairs. After 170 years of sporadic but steadily intensifying defiance, they finally overthrew imperial rule. The adoption of the Constitution and the election of Andrew Jackson as President completed the "grand design of Providence" and made the United States the political envy of the world. That hundreds of thousands of liberty-loving Americans had tried to keep the colonies within the empire in 1776 was a paradox that Bancroft did his best to ignore.

Scorning the notion of inborn emotions, a new school of historians led by Charles M. Andrews produced a torrent of books and articles in the early decades of the twentieth century, which ascribed the political behavior of colonial Americans to the influence of long-range, external developments. Revolutions, Andrews asserted in his presidential address to the American Historical Association in 1925, did not flow from individual decisions, because individuals were merely the agents of impersonal forces, the most potent of which was physical environment. In the case of the American Revolution, conditions in the colonies had generated new wants, new desires, new points of view, and finally a new order of society, which inevitably came into conflict with an empire which insisted on containing its colonies within a familiar order. But why did conditions in America not transform *all* its inhabitants into revolutionary agents? Andrews did not know, and the failure of his environmental determinism to account for the loyalists raised doubts about his interpretation of the patriots.

The first books to pay serious attention to internal disagreements in late-eighteenth-century America were Charles H. Lincoln's *The Revolutionary Movement in Pennsylvania* (1901), Carl L. Becker's *History of Political Parties in the Province of New York* (1909), and above all, Charles A. Beard's *An Economic Interpretation of the Constitution* (1913).[1] The conflicts between the business community and the rest of society, which characterized the era of Theodore Roosevelt and Woodrow Wilson, had alerted the authors of these books to the socioeconomic tensions of an earlier America. By the time Beard published his arresting analysis of the economic interests of the delegates to the Constitutional Convention, the Progressive historians had given their readers the sense that the entire period from 1760 to the adoption of the Constitution almost thirty years later had been marked by struggle between the unprivileged and the privileged. But it was not until Arthur M. Schlesinger, Sr., wrote his study of *The Colonial Merchants and the American Revolution* (1918) that the Progressive historians came fully to grips with the problem of the patriots and the loyalists. The merchants of the 1760s, Schlesinger said, considered the Sugar Act, the Stamp Act, and the Townshend Acts to be attacks on their livelihoods. They therefore made common cause with other colonists who wanted to see these regulations removed. To their horror, the merchants found that their own reasoned protests were being drowned out by the inflammatory oratory of radical demagogues and the answering roars of rioting mobs. Fearful of the violence and the leveling tendencies of these developments, the merchants reversed their strategy at the beginning of the 1770s and endeavored to play a mediating role in British-American relations. In 1773, however, the imposition of the Tea Act spurred the merchants to rejoin the resistance movement—but once again they lost control of it to more intransigent men. When the colonies finally declared their independence, the merchants faced a difficult choice. Some of them joined the rebellion. Others remained loyal. But the important point was that they all calculated the economic odds before deciding. "It should be recognized that, when the moment for the crucial decision came," Schlesinger cautioned, "the choice which every merchant had to make was not, and could not be, a mere mechanical one, premised upon strict considerations of an informed class interest. Like other human beings, his mind was affected or controlled by the powerful influences of temperament, environment, and tradition."[2] Yet in spite of this warning, Schlesinger's analysis left no doubt of his belief that the class-interest calculation was supremely important. Man was an economic animal, and the American Revolution had been the consequence of a long and complicated interplay of economic factors, involving conflicts within the colonies as well as antagonisms between the New World and the Old.

The analysis made sense. It explained the behavior of both the patriots and the loyalists. It fitted the class-conscious temper of twentieth-century politics. And in the 1920s and 1930s it swept the field of Revolutionary scholarship. J. Franklin Jameson, Allan Nevins, Vernon Louis Parrington, Merrill Jensen, and a host of other historians reiterated and elaborated the Schlesinger thesis, and as it entered the new textbooks of the period, it became the interpretation on which virtually all American schoolchildren were raised. No longer was there any mystery about who the patriots and the loyalists were, or why they had been on opposite sides. Farmers and small plantation owners from the "interior democracies" of the Southern Piedmont and the western sectors of the Middle Colonies and New England had joined with artisans, mechanics, and professional agitators in the cities in defiant protest against the policies of the imperial government and of the "ruling minorities" in their midst. The pressure of events then persuaded a substantial number of merchants and landed aristocrats to go along with the radicals, at which point war became inevitable. With the defeat of the British forces at Yorktown, the estates of the loyalist oligarchs were confiscated and some of them redistributed. In ensuing years, the suffrage was extended, primogeniture and entail were abolished, quitrents were done away with, and the Anglican church—the church of the loyalists—was disestablished. Growing up in the 1930s, I studied a textbook in school which made the differences between the loyalists and the patriots as clear-cut as the distinctions that

Franklin D. Roosevelt was drawing between economic royalists and the forgotten man.

Immediately before and after World War II, however, a series of specialized studies of provincial politics appeared which challenged the Manichaean model of the Schlesinger school. These books were the forerunners of the wholesale assault on the Progressives that was mounted by a new generation of scholars in the 1950s. It was wrong to say that struggles between the unprivileged and the privileged had dominated political life in colonial America, for as a score of local histories convincingly demonstrated, political affairs on every level in every colony had been effectively controlled by elites. Conflicts often arose within these elites, as various leaders and factions jockeyed for position, but personal ambition, not differing class interests, was the source of friction. Indeed, the very concept of class antagonism was called into question by the new investigators. For careers had been open to talent and class lines had been permeable in eighteenth-century America. While antagonisms between social groups sometimes became so bitter that they flared into violence, these outbursts were remarkable for their infrequency, and certainly bore little resemblance to the discontents of the French Revolution, to which some of the Progressive historians had compared them. In the fluid world epitomized by Benjamin Franklin's *Autobiography,* Americans had been in motion, geographically, socially, and economically, and their mobility made it extraordinarily difficult to fit them into categories and make them stay there.

It also proved difficult to relate the different political allegiances that Americans swore to in 1776 to regional, occupational, educational, religious, and ethnic classifications. Efforts were made in all of these areas, but the linkages achieved were maddeningly inconclusive. A majority of the loyalists were farmers, but a majority of farmers were patriots. Although royal (and proprietary) officials constituted the most predic-

tably pro-British part of colonial society, their ranks were far
from solid. Many doctors were loyalists; most teachers were
patriots; but neither side had anything like a monopoly of
either profession. Clergymen were divided, as were their parishioners, no matter whether they were Anglicans, Congrega-
tionalists, Baptists, Quakers, or Catholics. The Piedmont
was divided. Tidewater was divided. The town of Barnstable,
Massachusetts, was split half and half. Brothers were divided.
Merchant partners were divided. And a study of forty-seven
barristers who were practicing in Massachusetts in 1774 revealed that fifteen became ardent patriots, four reluctant patriots, nineteen ardent loyalists, eight reluctant loyalists, and
one kept his sentiments to himself. All of which proved very
little, except that lawyers were more likely to be loyalists than
were members of the general population, but not to a sufficient
degree to establish the hypothesis that membership in the legal
profession was the determinant of political choice.[3]

With the shattering of Schlesinger's socioeconomic synthesis,
historians turned to political and constitutional analysis, pro-
ducing such distinguished books as Edmund Morgan's history
of the Stamp Act crisis, Carl Ubbelohde's account of the changing role of the vice-admiralty courts, and Jack P. Greene's
study of the lower houses of assembly in the Southern royal
colonies. The weakness, however, of post-Progressive scholarship was that its practitioners no longer had a general theory
of colonial behavior that enabled them to explain the disunity
of Revolutionary America. If they concentrated their attention
on the behavior of the patriots, it was because they were at a
loss to understand why the loyalists had not behaved in the
same way. In the words of Jack P. Greene, the "guiding question" of the books written in the 1950s and early 1960s was
"why the colonists became unhappy enough in the years after
1763 to revolt."[4] The very fact that Greene referred to the
patriots as "the colonists" was an indication of how hard he
and other historians of the period had tried to forget the trouble-
some presence of the loyalists.

An entirely new dimension was added to Revolutionary scholarship in the mid-1960s, when Bernard Bailyn proposed that historians had been looking for the origins of the break with Britain in the wrong places. They had been racking every external event they could think of, in the hope that it might prove to have a causative significance. But they had not been looking inward, into the huge world of inner life, where the responses to events take shape. The minds of eighteenth-century Americans, Bailyn pointed out, had been exposed for generations to an ideology of virtue and corruption, derived from English sources which had been historically opposed to the governing style of the Junto Whigs, Walpole, and their successors. This peculiar configuration of conspiratorial ideas constituted in effect an "intellectual switchboard wired so that certain combinations of events would activate a distinct set of signals—danger signals, indicating hidden impulses and the likely trajectory of events impelled by them."[5] Twists and turns in imperial policy after 1763 were thus given a sinister interpretation by the colonists every time they occurred, and it was the transformation of real grievances into paranoiac fantasies of corruption and conspiracy which in the end propelled the Americans into revolution.

The Ideological Origins of the American Revolution (1967) was a path-breaking book. Yet for all its innovative brilliance, the book was overtitled, as two younger scholars, both of whom had studied under Bailyn, made clear in the early 1970s. While acknowledging the important role played by "Real Whig" ideology in the development of a revolutionary frame of mind in the American colonies, Pauline Maier pointed out that a conspiratorial view of the world was not the same thing as a decision to act, and hence could not be considered the origin of the Revolution. A belief in "Real Whig" ideology was not by itself a sufficient explanation of why the patriots took the revolutionary road, and it was not at all helpful in explaining why the loyalists refused to accompany them. It did not even serve to distinguish between the two groups,

Maier said, because a good many loyalists were ideologically in-
distinguishable from a Christopher Gadsden or a Sam Adams.
Mary Beth Norton, an expert on the Tory exiles in Britain,
reinforced Maier's comments about the loyalists by confess-
ing that she had not found anything that the Tory exiles had
in common other than their adherence to imperial rule. The
obvious implication of her statement was that the loyalists
were not bound together either by an immunity to "Real
Whig" ideology or by a belief in it.[6]

By calling attention to the failure of ideological analysis to
account for the loyalists, Maier and Norton eventually alerted
other readers to an even more serious gap in Bailyn's argument. How many patriots actually were persuaded that a
great conspiracy against traditional liberties was afoot in the
Anglo-American world? One hundred percent? Eighty percent? Sixty percent? *The Ideological Origins* asserted that "the
majority" of "American leaders" were true believers in the
conspiracy theory, but offered no substantiating proof of
this curiously guarded estimate.[7]

With the growing realization of the imperfections in Bailyn's
brilliant argument, there has recently been a revival of interest,
particularly among younger, politically radical historians, in
the socioeconomic motives of the colonists. Thus far, however,
nothing conclusive has come of this interest—to the surprise
of no one familiar with the rise and fall of the Schlesinger thesis.

Two hundred years, in sum, after the signing of the Declaration of Independence, historians are still not satisfied that
they understand the pre-Revolutionary differences between
the patriots and the loyalists, and they still cannot completely
explain why apparently like-minded neighbors went separate
ways in 1776. The startlingly high level of vituperation that
has marked recent conferences on the Revolution is a manifestation, in my opinion, of a massive professional frustration,
as well as of a superb intellectual energy.

But while the experts on the Revolution have been wrangling,
extremely interesting work has been going on, in another

part of the colonial forest, on early American family history. The historians engaged in this work have included Oscar and Mary Handlin, Philip J. Greven, Jr., John Demos, Daniel Scott Smith, Robert A. Gross, Kenneth A. Lockridge, Stephen Foster, T. H. Breen, and Robert Wells. Thanks to their researches, we now have a general understanding of the changes that took place in parent-child relations in the seventeenth and eighteenth centuries.

The colonists of seventeenth-century America sought to establish a stable, traditionally structured society. The cohesion of the community, not the liberation of the individual, was their goal. They were also convinced that family life was the key to everything they were trying to achieve. "Such as Families are, such at last the Church and Common-wealth must be," said James Fitch of Boston in 1683.[8]

Accordingly, bachelors in small New England towns were often taxed and ordered to join some stable household. Other colonial laws forbade children to disobey their parents, and even threatened flagrant offenders with the death penalty. The authority of fathers was further reinforced by their ownership of the limited amount of land that had been cleared for farming, and by their knowledge of the special skills essential for practicing a craft. Through their careful control of the transmission of wealth and knowledge, they maintained power over their sons even after the latter were grown up. As Philip J. Greven, Jr., observes in his careful study of four generations of families in Andover, Massachusetts, "the goals of order, hierarchy, and the closely-knit community" seemed to be within the reach of seventeenth-century Americans.[9]

In the last decades of the century, however, Andover's birth rate suddenly spurted, and was followed in ensuing decades by a slower but sustained population growth. By the middle years of the eighteenth century, the town no longer had enough land to absorb all its inhabitants. This meant that fathers could no longer exercise patriarchal control over their sons, because they no longer, in many instances, had anything to give them, while sons "reached maturity sooner, married younger, established their independence more effectively and earlier in life, and departed from the community with . . . greater frequency than in earlier generations." Richard Bushman has found a similarly dramatic population explosion in Connecticut. Between 1670 and 1700, the province's population grew by 58 percent; between 1700 and 1730 it expanded 380 percent. Although Robert Wells's study of family size among Pennsylvania Quakers suggests that demographic changes in the Middle Colonies were less drastic than in New England, it too shows a sharp rise in the number of children growing to maturity in the early eighteenth century.[10]

The growing economic prosperity of the colonies and the opening up of more and more remote areas for settlement also made for social instability after 1700. Sons who chafed under parental restraint found that they could solve their domestic problems simply by taking off for the greener pastures on the other side of family fences. Runaways, however, only dramatized a more general phenomenon: the length of time that eighteenth-century adolescent males were dependent on their parents had diminished in direct ratio to the increase of occupational opportunities for young men.[11]

Inevitably, the nature of family life changed. In the words of Oscar and Mary Handlin, the eighteenth-century father "retained authority at home over children while they were there, as over wife and servants, but the consciousness that his rule was temporary qualified his power, as did the dawning awareness that the proper rearing for boys was one that prepared them to go."[12] A boy might be on his own among adults by the age of thirteen, married at eighteen—as Patrick Henry was—and in command of a ship or a militia company before he was twenty-one. "Though not yet fourteen years of age, like other boys, I imagined myself almost a man," Andrew Sherburne recalled in his memoirs of his New Hampshire youth. After obtaining the consent of his father, the thirteen-year-old Andrew went to war against the British in 1779 in the crew of the continental ship of war *Ranger.* [13]

Parent-child relations in England, Scotland, and the West Indies were also evolving in these years. Eighteenth-century Britons were a rising people, no matter where they lived; in Aberdeen and Christiansted, no less than in Boston and Charleston, parents faced the problem of readying their sons for early departure from the family nest. Yet if the changes in family life had a transatlantic scope, they did not affect the experience of every young male in the English-speaking world. For while many parents brought up their sons in the new way, other parents either did not wish to do so, or were unable to. On the basis of my own analysis of Revolutionary biography as well as of the conclusions of other scholars, I would say that in the first half of the eighteenth century most parents responded to changing social conditions by granting their sons a considerable amount of freedom from early childhood onward, and by permitting them to have a vote in decisions affecting their own destiny. These families remained father-dominated; there was no doubt about that. But within the continuing requirement of respect for paternal authority there emerged a new—an unprecedented—respect for the individual rights of male children. At the same time, however, a substantial minority of parents did not conform, either by intention or accident, to the new style of parenting. In the majority of families, father-son relations were marked by a fruitful tension between childish freedom and adult authority; but in a good many other families, that tension was somehow lost or never achieved.

Except for a speculative sentence or two near the close of Philip Greven's study of Andover, historians of the colonial American family have steered clear of the question of whether the microstructure of parent-child relations between 1700 and 1750 had anything to do with the macrostructure of colonial-imperial relations between 1760 and 1776. Yet it could very well be that the two structures were related to one another, and that the political disunity of Revolutionary America was the climactic consequence of contrasting modes of upbringing.

The idea that family life had political implications would not have startled the colonists. As every educated member of the Revolutionary generation well knew, Hobbes and Filmer had both invoked the patriarchal family of seventeenth-century Britain as a model of the proper relationship between a monarch and his subjects. Locke, to be sure, had dismissed this sort of analogical reasoning as specious, and in the early eighteenth century American writers had regarded it as out of date. But in the 1760s, when the British suddenly imposed a stricter set of rules on the colonists than they had known for many decades, analogical reasoning came back into fashion with a vengeance. Because by cutting into the political, economic, and constitutional freedoms to which the colonists had long been accustomed, the British in effect were relegating them to the status of children in an old-fashioned patriarchal family. Arising out of this perception of their situation came a flood of personal memories, and a concerted effort on the part of patriot spokesmen to define the meaning of their lives. In their childhoods, they remembered, they had certainly known rules, but the rules had not been designed to bind them permanently to their parents or to break their spirit of independence. As a result, they had grown up very quickly; and in their maturity they had enjoyed, along with other freedoms, a high degree of autonomy in their dealings with imperial Britain.

These intertwining memories were then encapsulated in a metaphor. Britannia was a mother, and America was her daughter—who was now grown up. King George was a father, and the colonists were his sons—who had long since learned how to fend for themselves. Again and again, in rebuses, pamphlets, sermons, speeches, and satirical fables, colonial writers rang the changes on a recurrent theme. On the literal as well as the symbolic level, these outbursts of the American spirit were charged with meaning. Francis Hopkinson, for instance, spun out "A Pretty Story" in 1774:

> Once upon a time, a great while ago, there lived a certain Nobleman, who had long possessed a very valuable Farm, and had a great number of children and grandchildren. Besides the annual profits of his land, which were very considerable, he kept a large shop of goods; and being very successful in trade, he became, in process of time, exceeding rich and powerful, insomuch that all his neighbors feared and respected him. With respect to the management of his family, it was thought he had adopted the most perfect mode that could be devised; for he had been at the pains to examine the economy of all his neighbors, and had selected from their plans all such parts as appeared to be equitable and beneficial, and omitted those which from experience were found to be inconvenient. Or, rather, by blending their several constitutions together, he had so ingeniously counterbalanced the evils of one mode of government with the benefits of another, that the advantages were richly enjoyed, and inconveniences scarcely felt. In short, his family was thought to be the best ordered of any in his neighborhood. . . .
>
> Now it came to pass that this Nobleman had, by some means or other, obtained a right to an immense tract of wild uncultivated country at a vast distance from his mansion house. But he set little store by this acquisition, as it yielded him no profit; nor was it likely to do so, being not only difficult of access on account of the distance, but was also overrun with innumerable wild beasts very fierce and savage,—so that it would be extremely dangerous to attempt taking possession of it.
>
> In process of time, however, some of his children, more stout and enterprising than the rest, requested leave of their Father to go and settle on this distant tract of land. Leave was readily obtained; but before they set out, certain agreements were stipulated between them. The principal were—the old Gentleman, on his part, engaged to protect and defend the

adventurers in their new settlements; to assist them in chasing away the wild beasts; and to extend to them all the benefits of the government under which they were born,—assuring them that although they should be removed so far from his presence, they should nevertheless be considered as the children of his family, and treated accordingly. At the same time, he gave each of them a bond for the faithful performance of these promises, in which, among other things, it was covenanted that they should each of them, in their several families, have a liberty of making such rules and regulations for their own good government as they should find convenient, provided the rules and regulations should not contradict or be inconsistent with the general standing orders established in his Farm. In return for these favors, he insisted that they, on their parts, should at all times acknowledge him to be their Father; that they should not deal with their neighbors without his leave, but send to his shop only for such merchandise as they should want. But in order to enable them to pay for such goods as they should purchase, they were permitted to sell the product of their lands to certain of his neighbors.

Having duly adjusted all these preliminaries, the hardy sons of the old Nobleman set off on their journey. After dangers and hardships without number, they at last got comfortably settled on the New Farm; in due time their harvests became abundant; and, keeping up a constant correspondence with the family on the Old Farm, they went to great expense for wagons, horses, and drivers, with which to bring from their Father's shop such goods as they wanted, which they paid for out of the produce of their lands. Thus matters went on very happily until, in an evil day, the old Nobleman's Wife [*i.e.*, the British Parliament] began to cast an avaricious eye upon the new settlers. In the first place, she issued an edict setting forth that, whereas the tailors of her family were greatly injured by the people of the New Farm, inasmuch as they presumed to make their own clothes, whereby the said tailors were deprived of the benefit of their custom, it was therefore ordained that for the future, the new settlers should not be permitted to have amongst them any shears or scissors, larger than a certain fixed size. In consequence of this, our adventurers were compelled to have their clothes made by their Father's tailors; but out of regard to the old Gentleman, they patiently submitted to this grievance. Next, she proceeded to lay heavy taxes upon them on various pretences, all the time receiving the fruits of their industry with both hands. Moreover, she persuaded her Husband to send amongst them, from time to time, a number of the most lazy and useless of his servants, under the specious pretext of defending them in their settlements, and of assisting to destroy the wild beasts, but in fact, to rid his own house of their company, not having employment for them, and at the same time to be a watch and a check upon the people of the New Farm.[14]

Relentlessly, past the Hat Act, the Stamp Act, the Tea Act, and the Boston port bill, Hopkinson proceeded through the litany of American grievances. The story was ridiculously crude and unsubtle, yet it established its author, as Moses Coit Tyler has observed, "as one of the three leading satirists on the Whig side of the American Revolution."[15] What made the story effective was that it drew upon two different realms of memory in the same breath. Hopkinson's admirers had a sense of what their lives meant, thanks to the self-consciousness which had been triggered by the new British rules. They warmed to "A Pretty Story" because the author combined a nostalgic recollection of a good relationship between a father and his sons with a proud recapitulation of the mutually respectful arrangements which had been worked out between the colonies and the Crown authority. Thus the sea change in imperial policy was an insult in more ways than one. It degraded the meaning of the colonists' early lives, and it did violence to the historic relationship between America and Britain. What "A Pretty Story" lacked in finesse, it made up for in double-barreled resentment.

Colonial defenders of Great Britain also resorted to the parent-child comparison in their polemics, but with an empha-

sis on continuing parental control that harked back to an
older style of child rearing. "Are we," asked the Tory Daniel
Leonard, "to take up arms and make war against our parent,
lest that parent, contrary to her own genius, inclination, affection, and interest, should treat us or our posterity as bastards, and not as sons, and instead of protecting, should en-
slave us? The annals of the world have not yet been deformed
with a single instance of so unnatural, so causeless, so wanton,
so wicked, a rebellion." In Sam Adams' view, however, Americans were already being treated "as bastards and not Sons,"
and John Adams was equally impatient with the idea that the
recalcitrant behavior of children was an adverse reflection on
them, rather than on their tyrannical parents:

> Have not children a right to complain when their parents are
> attempting to break their limbs, to administer poison, or to
> sell them to enemies for slaves? Let me entreat you to con-
> sider, will the mother be pleased when you represent her as
> deaf to the cries of her children—when you compare her to
> the infamous miscreant who lately stood on the gallows for
> starving her child,—when you resemble her to Lady Macbeth
> in Shakespeare (I cannot think of it without horror) who
>
>> Had given suck, and knew
>> How tender 't was to love the babe that milked her,
>> but yet who could
>> even while 't was smiling in her face,
>> Have plucked her nipple from the boneless gums,
>> and dashed the brains out.

Thomas Paine, with his polemical skills, gave the parent-
child analogy an even more memorable formulation. "To
know whether it be the interest of this continent to be independent, we need only ask this easy simple question: Is it the
interest of a man to be a boy all his life?" No American who
heard that taunting question ever forgot it. As he talked to an
Indian chief about the causes of the Revolution, five years

after the war had begun, Thomas Jefferson echoed Paine's psychopolitical language when he explained that "Our forefathers were Englishmen, inhabitants of a little island beyond the great water, and, being distressed for land, they came and settled here. As long as we were young and weak, the English, whom we had left behind, made us carry all our wealth to their country, to enrich them; and, not satisfied with this, they at length began to say we were their slaves, and should do whatever they ordered us. We were now grown up and felt ourselves strong; we knew we were free as they were, . . . and were determined to be free as long as we should exist. For this reason they made war on us." In Jefferson's view, no less than in Paine's or Hopkinson's, growing up was the means by which boys became independent of their fathers.[16]

In the writings of their own spokesmen, then, the patriots and the loyalists called attention to the interrelationship of private and public experience. Historians who equate professional rigor with narrowness, and who have broken down the study of the past into airtight compartments, could learn a lot about the practice of their profession from the men who made and opposed the American Revolution.

Notes

1. I am indebted in this paragraph to Jack P. Greene's informative bibliographical essay, *The Reappraisal of the American Revolution in Recent Historical Literature* (Washington, 1967), pp. 8-17.

2. Arthur M. Schlesinger, *The Colonial Merchants and the American Revolution, 1763-1776* (New York, 1939), pp. 602-03. [Originally published 1918.]

3. Wallace Brown, *The Good Americans. The Loyalists in the American Revolution* (New York, 1969), pp. 2-29. Francis T. Bowles, "The Loyalty of Barnstable in the Revolution," *Publications of the Colonial Society of Massachusetts*, 25 (1922-1924), pp. 265-345. ohn M. Murrin, "The Legal Transformation: The Bench and Bar of Eighteenth-Century Massachusetts," in Stanley N. Katz, ed.,

Colonial America: Essays in Politics and Social Development (Boston, 1971), pp. 415-49.

4. Greene, p. 32.

5. Bernard Bailyn, *The Ideological Origins of the American Revolution* (Cambridge, Mass., 1967), pp. 22-23.

6. Pauline Maier, *From Resistance to Revolution* (New York, 1972), p. xv. Mary Beth Norton, *The British-Americans. The Loyalist Exiles in England, 1774-1789* (Boston, 1972), p. 8.

7. Bailyn, p. 22.

8. Quoted in Philip J. Greven, Jr., *Four Generations: Population, Land and Family in Colonial Andover, Massachusetts* (Ithaca, 1970), n.p.

9. *Ibid.*, pp. 270-72.

10. *Ibid.* Richard L. Bushman, *From Puritan to Yankee: Character and the Social Order in Connecticut, 1690-1765* (Cambridge, Mass., 1967), p. 83. Robert Wells, "Family Size and Fertility Control in Eighteenth-Century America: A Study of Quaker Families," *Population Studies,* XXV (1971).

11. Oscar Handlin and Mary F. Handlin, *Facing Life. Youth and the Family in American History* (Boston, 1971), pp. 12-17.

12. *Ibid.*, p. 18.

13. Robert H. Bremner, ed., *Children and Youth in America. A Documentary History* (Cambridge, Mass., 1970), I, p. 141.

14. These paragraphs of intermingled quotation and summary are taken from Moses Colt Tyler, *The Literary History of the American Revolution, 1763-1783* (New York, 1897), I, pp. 281-84.

15. *Ibid.*, p. 291.

16. *Ibid.*, pp. 97-98, 365. [John Adams and Daniel Leonard], *Novanglus and Massachusettensis* (Boston, 1819), p. 145. John C. Miller, *Sam Adams. Pioneer in Propaganda* (Boston, 1936), p. 273. John Adams, "A Dissertation on the Canon and Feudal Law [1765]," reprinted in *The Works of John Adams,* ed. C. F. Adams (Boston, 1850-1856), III, pp. 448-64. Thomas Paine, *The Writings of Thomas Paine,* ed. Moncure D. Conway (New York, 1894-1896), I, p. 203. Dumas Malone, *Jefferson the Virginian* (Boston, 1948), p. 225. See also Edwin G. Burrows and Michael Wallace, "The American Revolution: The Ideology and Psychology of National Liberation," *Perspectives in American History,* VI (1972), pp. 167-306.

Afterword

Speaking for his older brothers as well as for himself, Senator Edward M. Kennedy has testified that "My father was a motivating, dominating, powerful force with very high expectations—especially for his sons. . . . You felt powerful demands on you."[1] To what extent did the celebrated "style" of the Kennedy Administration reflect the efforts of three permanently awestruck sons to live up to the swashbuckling exploits of the Dreiserian titan who had sired them?

Lyndon B. Johnson learned early from his mother that love was conditional on performance. Were her demands on him, and his eagerness to satisfy them, the source of his curious comparison of America to a beautiful woman, who would grow fatter and fatter as a result of his Great Society programs?[2]

If we had the patience, and the wit, to link historical events with massive accumulations of information about personal backgrounds, the political culture of our own time might become more understandable, too. Such as families are, such at last the commonwealth must be.

Notes

1. Quoted in James Stevenson, "A Reporter at Large," *The New Yorker*, August 25, 1975, p. 69. Kennedy's words were originally quoted by his mother, Rose Fitzgerald Kennedy, in her autobiography, *Times to Remember*.

2. Speech by Doris Kearns, Federal City Club, Washington, D.C., *Washington Post*, June 16, 1976, pp. B1, B16.

Index

About the Author

Kenneth S. Lynn, professor of history at Johns Hopkins University, specializes in American literature and intellectual history. His previous works include *The Dream of Success, Mark Twain and Southwestern Humor, William Dean Howells: An American Life,* and *Visions of America* (Greenwood Press, 1973).